PROTECTIVE DISCRIMINATION

About the Editor

Dr. A.K. Lal is a sociologist of repute having three decades of experience in research and training. Dr. Lal has worked on different themes and has successfully completed projects funded by the Central Government as well as Voluntary Organizations. He has special interests in the problems of the weaker sections which finds articulation in his contributions facilitating understanding of the phenomenon of change and continuity among these people. He has long experience of field work in Bihar, Haryana, Madhya Pradesh, Delhi and Uttar Pradesh. Dr. Lal has been in close rapport with sociological activities of Sulabh International and has been founder Director of its institutions for research and social intervention. He also worked as senior Fellow, G.B. Pant Social Science Institute, Allahabad for two years. Dr. Lal has authored a number of books including the well known work on Bonded Labours in Bihar entitled *Politics of Poverty*. His other books are *The Urban Family, Elite and Development* (with Sachchidananda), *Harijan Elite* (with Sachchidananda), *Dalits in Action* and *Secularism Concept and Practice*. Dr. Lal is presently a Reader in the A.N. Sinha Institute of Social Studies, Patna.

PROTECTIVE DISCRIMINATION
Ideology and Praxis

A.K. LAL
A.N. Sinha Institute of Social Studies, Patna

Published for
G.B. PANT SOCIAL SCIENCE INSTITUTE, ALLAHABAD
by
CONCEPT PUBLISHING COMPANY, NEW DELHI-110059

ISBN 81-7022-933-2

First Published 2002

Published and Printed by
Ashok Kumar Mittal
Concept Publishing Company
A/15-16, Commercial Block, Mohan Garden
New Delhi-110059 (INDIA)

Phones: 5648039, 5649024
Fax: 091-11-5648053
Email: publishing@conceptpub.com.

FOREWORD

State policy favouring preferential treatment to the weaker sections of the society has fairly long existence in India. Initiated to provide succour to the deprived communities occupying the base of the traditional stratification system even now it constitutes the most important strategy to alleviate the depressed section of the society from the morass of degradation. Its impact has been profound as it has contributed significantly towards the empowerment of these people. In the process it has, however, led to unintended consequences especially by promoting differential development among the scheduled communities. With the passage of time it has also undergone modifications to accommodate new interests asserting for compensatory discrimination. Such claims that tend to be proliferating has enhanced the demand-load on the scarce resources of the State. While initiatives are needed to ensure its wider reach among the more deserving and neglected, its use as a tool to serve selfish political interest deserve expert scrutiny. We also need to discuss the desirability of its indefinite stay especially as the exclusive solvent to the problems of uneven development.

With these aims in view the G.B. Pant Social Science Institute organised a seminar inviting papers on this issue of urgent social interest. The present work includes the papers presented at the seminar. We also sponsored research articles on the issue subsequently from the known experts for inclusion in the volume and have tried to ensure a rounded perspective on the theme. On behalf of the Institute and on my own behalf I wish to thank the contributors for their kind support in preparation of the book. Dr. A.K. Lal who initiated this project on behalf of the Institute and prepared the book for wider diffusion of the dialogue on the issue deserve our appreciations. I would be failing in my duty if I don't acknowledge the support rendered by Shri Ashok Kumar Mittal of the Concept Publishing Company, New Delhi for his personal interest in ensuring timely publication of the book. We are obliged to the Indian Council of Social Science Research which provided financial support for the conduct of the seminar.

PROF. JANAK PANDY
Director
G.B. Pant Social Science Institute,
Allahabad

CONTENTS

LIST OF CONTRIBUTORS

K.N. Bhatt is Research Associate in Economics, G.B. Pant Social Science Institute, New Delhi.

Arundhuti Roy Choudhury is Research Fellow, Indian Social Institute, New Delhi.

Walter Fernandes is the Programme Director, Programme for Tribal Studies Indian Social Institute, New Delhi.

A.K. Lal is Reader in Political Science, A.N. Sinha Institute of Social Studies, Patna.

Jitendra Narayan is Reader in Political Science, L.N. Mithila University, Darbhanga, Bihar.

Sudha Pai is Associate Professor, Centre for the Study of Political Systems, Jawahar Lal Nehru University, New Delhi.

S.K. Pant is Reader in Economics, G.B. Pant Social Science Institute, Allahabad.

Rajalaxmi Rath is Research Scientist (UGC), A.N. Sinha Institute of Social Studies, Patna.

Professor Sachchidananda is the Director, Sulabh Institute of Development Studies, Patna.

Professor R.R. Singh is Professor and Head, Department of Social Work, Delhi University, Delhi.

Shailendra K. Tiwary is Junior Research Fellow, Department of Political Science, University of Allahabad.

R.M. Tripathi is Research Associate in Geography, G.B. Pant Social Science Institute, Allahabad.

Jose Vadasery is a Research Scholar (Sociology), A.N. Sinha Institute of Social Studies, Patna.

INTRODUCTION

Protective discrimination seeks to offset systematic and cumulative deprivation. It comprises compensatory programmes to lift the deprived and exploited communities. Preferment is available to ensure a share of power and opportunity to the historically disadvantaged to promote their advancement until "they can hold their own without it". It thus represents a legislative device to steer the process of mobility among the depressed classes. It intends to ensure dispersal of inequality and is wedded to remove obstacles to change in favour of the exploited and the oppressed. The affirmative State action constitutes a radical option to initiate a process of reallocation of resources on an egalitarian basis. Compensatory programmes aim at helping socially degraded and economically marginalised communities by retaining resources in the emerging opportunity structure in their favour. Special measures of redressal are needed to compensate such sections of the society that remain constrained on account of inherited deprivation.

Initiated to help the scheduled castes and the scheduled tribes, the policy subsequently has acquired an extended clientele. Within its sweep are now included not only the exteriors and insulated but also those located at the periphery. Its extension in the present context reflects the response of the State to prevent continued appropriation of the resources by the entrenched few. Continued negligence of certain sections in spite of intents for their elevation led the recently raised to assert for extension of protective discrimination in their favour. Thus pressures of the cognate caste groups located at the middle of the traditional stratification system led to its extension. It enabled them to seek a fit between their elevated status in the power structure and available resources in the prevalent opportunity structure. The stigmatized communities are not the only concern of the State policy for affirmative action as other sections are also incorporated among its beneficiaries and many more are claiming for their inclusion. We are today a nation with comprehensive system of preferential treatment offering different benefits to divergent groups of people. Initiated as a short-term measure protective discrimination seems poised to perpetuate indefinitely. Pressures of new segments aspiring for inclusion have accorded unprecedented resilience and inclusiveness to the policy. It has an encompassing application.

Affirmative State benefits are available to ensure effective participation of segments that remained unrepresented in politics and governance. Its application has ushered a breakthrough in a situation favouring perpetuation of inequality and stagnation. It has made possible 'coming up' of the lowest from a state of hopelessness. Various attributes of status no longer congrue to inhibit their advance. Positions in the diversified opportunity structure are no longer the exclusive privilege of the limited few. Elite are being recruited from different social strata. Conceived for the benefit of the depressed communities the policy however seems to favour limited individuals and their families as benefits remain stuck up at the top. Downward percolation and wider horizontal dispersal of its benefits tend to be elusive. Then situation of conflicting aspirations has led to clash of interests leaving the needy and deserving unprotected. Unwarranted distortions have often defeated the purpose for which it was conceived. Egalitarianism aspired through protective discrimination seems to have accentuated cleavages also. Polarization around caste identities is sharp. Its clientele are decided more on account of political compulsions rather than for social concern. It also seems to have accelerated the process of differential development within the target group as the weakest among the weak remain deprived and neglected. Its implementation seems to be skewed in favour of caste and class.

We need to seek an expert discussion on its usefulness in different sectors and at diverse levels among different communities. Distortions and lapses in implementation of this policy have to be identified to suggest their needed ratification. The future implications of unbridled proliferation in aspirations for State protection are to be studied. Policy contents and methodological details to assess the entitlement for such benefits are to be worked out.

Initiating the dialogue on relevance of protective discrimination as a strategy for change and empowerment Walter Fernandes maintains that the policy owes its origin to the feeling of guilt among the dominant castes over the cruelty that the subaltern encountered since time immemorial. Its arrival is attributed to the dominant castes' need for numbers in order to perpetuate themselves in the emerging power structure. It was oriented to seek their integration within the dominant mainstream as non-protesting appendage. Such initiatives also turned out to be inadequate for reduction of inherited inequality as capital-intensive and sophisticated technology based pattern of development further marginalised them in absence of a social base seeking investment in their favour. Non-existence of an elaborate social policy for needed upliftment of the deprived enabled the ruling class to prevent downward percolation of available facilities to the deserving. Since social transformation remained elusive only a few among the historically disadvantaged could have the enabling resources to claim the benefits. Shift in locus of power in favour of the landowning middle castes seems to have turned the situation for worse as they tend to be selfish and ruthless exploiters. Fernandes pleads for continuation of reservation in favour of the scheduled castes to enable them to compete with those that are traditionally privileged in the matter of resource endowment. He expresses the need for such modifications in the policy outline that could ensure even spread and priority attention. Provisions are to be made to make it effective for the lowest among the lowly and steps are needed to exclude those who are in no need of it. Policies oriented to prepare social base for eradication of poverty are needed to lift the deprived with the help of protective discrimination. He feels the need for evolution of a social policy in this regard to eradicate poverty and to facilitate the participation of the deprived as equal partners in development.

Sachchidananda maintains that the policy of protective discrimination has facilitated selective appropriation of benefits among the limited sections. Leadership produced in the wake of implementation of policies of protective discrimination tends to be unresponsive to the community of its origin. They are unable to federate themselves into a pressure group seeking effective implementation of the welfare and development schemes. He feels that competing interests of leadership have rendered these people disorganized and split. He makes a plea for looking at the parameters of backwardness in a dynamic perspective to facilitate its availability for the most deserving. Studies on the impact of protective discrimination on the scheduled castes reveal that there is a need to exclude undeserving individuals and developed castes from the schedule incorporating castes for special protection. Such steps he feels are necessary to reduce resentment against reservation and to encourage private initiatives in support of the deprived and neglected. Widening of opportunities and inculcation of appropriate skills to avail due placement are mentioned as necessary conditions for the development of the historically deprived and social stigmatised.

R.R. Singh's paper elaborates the substantive and procedural aspects of protective discrimination with special reference to the scheduled castes. He finds that the strategies to eliminate dysfunctionality of the stratified traditional system under the compensatory discrimination programme have led to unintended consequences seeking effective intervention for proper rectification. Sensitivity and responsiveness to promote equality notwithstanding State's response to encounter inequality remains inadequate. Programmes of affirmative action need the support of the civil society in order to be effective. Inherited constraints in order to be reduced seek constant support of compensatory inputs. Legislative enactments for their proper implementation require popular support. He feels the need for eligibility determining indicators to scientifically identify the target groups in need of such support.

A.K. Lal suggests to have a fresh look at the provisions of protective discrimination to come out of the tangled skein in which the country finds itself placed. He feels the need for a social policy that could ensure a better fit between deprivation and protective support. Weighted index of backwardness is suggested to be evolved to determine disadvantages for individual cases. Exit system to exclude the privileged is suggested to be evolved. Institutional and procedural safeguards have to be strengthened to stem distortions. Reservation in spite of being an unavoidable necessity is unworthy of acquiring an unlimited spread. It has to be a secondary option to be used as a support for the essential strategies for structural social transformation.

Sudha Pai describes the initiatives of the Bahujan Samaj Party as dominant constituent in power structure towards the empowerment of *dalits*. Its ideological thrust and strategies to empower *dalits* are accorded detailed elaboration. Policies aimed at ameliorating the condition of *dalits* and their execution under the *dalit* leadership find scrutiny to illustrate the scope of State intervention in lifting the deprived and the oppressed from the morass of degradation. Their studies indicate that programmes for empowerment have better chances of success among the conscious and assertive. Inert and dependence-oriented lag behind leading to alienation and discontent. Conflict to claim State-owned resources for social welfare is inimical to emergence of *dalits* as a corporate identity. Selective appropriation that follows restricted percolation of such benefits leads to perpetuation of discriminations.

S.K. Pant maintains that post-independence measures for the amelioration of the poor in spite of the impressive economic growth have been of little benefit to the deprived as beneficiaries of the trickle-down effect. Education tends to have a sparse spread among these people keeping them unfit to find suitable location in the diversified occupational structure. Poverty alleviation programmes appear externally imposed making them more dependent. He is of the opinion that the policy of protective discrimination represents the only systematic and effective strategy of support to these people. It seems to have enabled the deprived to seek redemption from fetters of exploitation enabling them to seek a suitable alteration in their existing conditions.

Raj Mani Tripathi in his paper elaborates the existing pattern of dispersal in the population of the scheduled castes and indicates the demographic, social and economic correlates. Programmes for bringing out change in these people are detailed. Tripathi finds the policy of protective discrimination most effective. It seems to have facilitated social and economic upliftment leading to the emergence of an elite from among these sections of the population. He maintains that the impressive achievements notwithstanding much remain to be done.

Rajalaxmi Rath is of the opinion that reservations have ushered profound alteration in the outlook of the scheduled castes. Substantial change in their economic status is attributed to their sponsored entry in the opportunity-structure. Social acceptability however does not seem to have acquired the dimension intended. Situation of status incongruence prevails on account of the prevalent lag between recently acquired secular identity and inherited social identity. Rath concludes that limitations notwithstanding compensatory discrimination have ushered alterations in favour of the scheduled castes.

Jose Vadasery details the impact of State support in the spread of education among the scheduled castes. He indicates that distortions and insensitivity have led to uneven spread of benefits. Compensatory provisions he feels have been cornered by the dominant section of the people. The incentives available under programmes to stir the mobility of *dalits* have been by and large ineffective in helping the overwhelming majority leaving them under conditions of staggering poverty. Problems of stagnation and failure in competition lead to increased inferiorization of *dalits*. Caste remains the overriding determinant to shape their interaction with teachers and students in the institutions of learning. Success in studies eludes them on account of economic constraints. He feels that *dalit*-friendly curriculum and conducive social context are necessary conditions for the success of protective discrimination programmes. In order to reduce the negative impact of the dual education policy on *dalits* reservation is sought in their favour in private educational institutions. He advocates the need to control the spread of elite educational institutions.

Arundhuti Roy Choudhury regards women's presence in political sphere to be a necessary condition for their empowerment. State initiatives in this regard are necessary for transforming a loosely formal democracy into a substantive democracy. It is required to weaken the patriarchal value framework and to bring gender at the centre stage of the national development process. Conceived to accelerate the process of socio-economic change and development the provisions seeking approval of the Parliament initiatives to ensure the representation of women represent a new height in the field of gender equality. It is an important policy outline to facilitate female emancipation from the fetters of subordination. Denial of such entitlement would render the society more iniquitous, less participatory and less democratic. Need for special mechanism to ensure due space to all strata of women in the power structure is expressed. Since gender relations are mediated through caste hierarchy transformative remedies have to be resorted to correct inequitable outcome of social arrangement. Roy Choudhury considers mobilisation of women necessary for integration of the diverse interests leading ultimately to the attainment of the unaccomplished aspirations of gender equality.

K.N. Bhatt examines the relevance of the State policy of reservation for the intermediate castes in the districts of Uttarakhand. Extension of facilities of compensatory discrimination in an area with sparse existence of such population is questioned. Bhatt maintains that such initiatives are oriented to increase the disadvantages of the people inhabiting the region. Sincere and comprehensive schemes to develop the region are more important than arrival of new exploiters under the protection of the reservation scheme. Tensions and unrest in the underdeveloped regions manifest the response of the inhabitants from these areas against State indifference to their aspirations for development and are indicative of their opposition to politically inspired strategies for social transformation.

Shailendra Kumar Tiwary focusses his paper to the thinking of Dr. B.R. Ambedkar especially with regard to the need for protective discrimination to the scheduled castes. Tiwary maintains that Ambedkar favoured protective discrimination as a strategy to rid certain sections of society from the traditionally legitimised exploitation. It was needed to support a social order based on justice and utility. Protective discrimination to Ambedkar was essential to establish the principle of equality and fraternity. He pleaded for spread of education among the deprived to ensure their proper development. He demanded a *swaraj* constitution to ensure a shift in power in favour of the scheduled castes enabling them to initiate steps needed for their own development.

Jitendra Narayan discusses the relevance of the constitutional provisions for protective discrimination to sponsor the mobility of the scheduled castes. Their effectiveness as a mechanism to help them come out of age-long suppression enabling the society to reshape itself on an egalitarian basis finds elaboration. Their presence as a safeguard to protect the interests of the underprivileged is detailed. Narayan feels that these legally recognized, constitutionally established, administratively enforced, judicially protected and politically supported provisions in spite of their utility require a fresh look to facilitate a cost-free social transformation.

A.K. LAL

1

RESERVATIONS AS A TOOL OF SOCIAL CHANGE

WALTER FERNANDES

The Gujarat riots of 1985, the anti-Mandal agitation of 1990 and the Supreme Court stand on the creamy layer have reopened the controversy around the issue of reservations. Some, particularly persons from the dominant classes, claim that reservations go against the principle of equality or that they bring down standards. Some, on the other side, state that the standards have been set by the dominant castes that have monopolised all benefits of development and have used education, high status jobs and other tools of upward mobility to keep themselves in power. As such, caste should be the only criterion of reservations.

We shall, therefore, look at the reservations not in order to refute any of these arguments, but to see whether they are the real or the only solution to the ongoing marginalisation of the subalterns. In this search, we take for granted the findings of other scholars that what are today known as the Scheduled Castes and Tribes have been discriminated against for centuries and have been deprived of equal opportunities. In thus accepting this starting point, we reject the stand of those who claim that reservations go against the principle of equality. We believe that inverse discrimination is required in favour of those who have been denied equality for centuries. The question we are asking is whether reservations as implemented today are adequate to overcome the disadvantaged state of these classes.

Reservations and Social Guilt

To find an answer to this question, one has to go back to the history of reservations. Their first feature is that that they originated from a feeling of guilt among the dominant castes that led the freedom movement, about the treatment meted out to the subaltern castes. These groups had lost their social and political power to the colonialists who occupied India for its economic exploitation but legitimised their enterprise in the name of the foreigner's mission of civilising education. While the colonialist presented India as a country of uncivilised people, in many cases, the missionary spoke of the caste-based Hindu society as unjust, as such destructive of the subalterns.[1] To this is to be added the resurgence among sections of *dalits* and tribals. As a result, in the late 19th and early 20th centuries, a relatively large number of *dalits* joined Christianity, Islam, Sikhism and other religions that gave them some hope of freedom from caste.[2] Many tribals were migrating towards Christianity in search of a new identity. Already from the 18th century, several other tribes rose in revolt against the British and the *Zamindars*. Most of their struggles were in defence of their livelihood and identity, both of which came under attack from the colonialist.[3]

Among others, these developments put the dominant classes on the defensive or produced in them a feeling of guilt. This interaction is at the basis of the reservation policy that was first promulgated in the Government of India Act of 1935 and later in the Indian Constitution. The 1930s when this policy was first formulated, were also the years when the main battle in the freedom movement was around the communal electorate. Numbers meant political power. The dominant castes could not afford to lose the *dalits* to other religions. They had to be preserved for the Hindu fold.[4] Thus the basic feature of the present reservation policy is that it originated more out of the dominant caste need for numbers and to defend their culture as egalitarian, than as a response to subaltern demands. Consequently, its orientation is welfare or relief. The caste system was not questioned, though untouchability was abolished. It was assumed in this measure that within a few years the subalterns would reach the standard of the high castes. The effort was to integrate them within the 'dominant mainstream' and not transform society. Power relations would not change. The basis of inequality was not questioned. The subalterns would have to be co-opted into the system.

This approach has also to be situated within the pattern of development chosen after independence. The constitutional privileges were introduced in the context of the process of modernisation of India required for national development. It was a capital-intensive and sophisticated technology based pattern. The assumption in this approach was that modernisation and technology would solve the social problems. The technology and other inputs chose persons with high literary and skills. The Scheduled Classes that had very limited access to literacy could not cope with this thrust towards an industrial infrastructure. The social sector did not receive adequate attention. Investment was certainly made on educational and health institutions. But they were only made available. Access to them was not ensured to the groups that had till then been kept down by the dominant classes. No effort was made to transform the unequal society. It was not realised that modernisation introduced in an unequal society intensifies inequalities rather than reducing them.[5] The strategy was to increase demand through investment in basic industries. It foundered because it—

> did not postulate the possibility that some producers in our economic system have the power to convert any increase in demand to profits for themselves first by competing out other producers (in which they get the co-operation of a section of the consumers) and then by deliberately restricting output. The clever and sophisticated strategy of the second plan meant to increase growth and reduce inequalities, ended up by increasing inequalities.[6]

The East Asian Model

In that sense, Indian policy was considerably different from that of Malaysia and many East Asian countries. In some form or the other, the latter set of countries combined an industrial with a social infrastructure. The Bhumiputra policy of Malaysia is an example. The situation of the Malays was analogous to that of the Indian *dalits*. They constituted around 60 per cent of the country's population. But economic power was concentrated in the hands of the Chinese and most workers were of Indian origin. Thus Malays were excluded from the benefits of development. Things reached a flash point with Singapore declaring independence from the federation in 1966 and the anti-Chinese riots in 1969. The Bhumiputra policy was a response to their demands and not a welfare measure. As in India, the Malaysian policy too had reservations. But unlike in India, it was only one of its components. In that component too, it went beyond the Indian policy in the sense that a certain percentage of posts had to be reserved for the Malays at every level, in the public as well as the private sector while in India it is limited to the public sector. More importantly, massive investments were made in the education, health, nutrition and hygiene of the Malays. In other words, while the Indian policy limited itself to making educational and health institutions and jobs available, the Malaysian system went beyond it to make them accessible to the Malays by building a social infrastructure.

Similar, to a great extent, was the approach of many East Asian countries that have today come to be known as Asian Tigers. Unlike in India that concentrated on building an industrial infrastructure, these countries combined the social with the industrial. The two Koreas, the two Chinas, Sukarno's Indonesia and Singapore made massive investments in universal education, health services and nutrition of the masses. Unlike in India they did not limit themselves to making institutions available. They went beyond it to ensure everybody's access to the infrastructure. Thus industrialisation of the country went hand in hand with the formation of skilled workers and consumers who had the purchasing power to keep the economy going. One can state that it was a capitalist system of ensuring a market and of training workers. But the reality is that unlike in India, at least a few benefits of development reached the majority of the population.

Ignoring the Poor

That gives one the main features of the Indian system. The country lacks a social policy. It limits itself to welfare. For example, education consists of making institutions available. But studies have shown that the socio-economic situation of the *dalits* and tribals prevents them from attending school. For example, in many regions, landlords—

> attach a great deal of importance to literacy and force it on their young ones, both male and female, they have purposely not cooperated with the authorities in the opening of a primary school in the village. They do not want Harijans to have access to education. When the members of the Youth Club proposed a primary school for the village, their elders snubbed them by pointing out the implications of education, the awakening that it will lead to, and the resultant consequences when the Harijans may either stop working....or demand higher wages or better conditions of work.[7]

But no effort is made in India to change this situation of lack of access. Education remains unchanged since the colonial times. This system based on full-time teaching and (high fees if it is in private schools and of good quality) excludes children from the subaltern classes who are needed at home either to look after their siblings or to work full time to supplement the meagre income of their parents. Such children belong mainly to the urban and rural poor, particularly the 'low castes'. Besides, the culture and curricula of educational institutions are geared to middle class needs. So many poor children drop out for economic reasons even if they join school in class 1.[8] One can see some signs of this situation in the 1991 census. It shows that against a literacy rate of 52 per cent in the general population, among the *dalits* it is only 37.2 per cent in the country as a whole, and about 23 per cent in States like Uttar Pradesh. That the future too is not bright can be seen from the fact that only about 76 per cent of *dalit* and a smaller number of tribal children enter school. Dropout rate is very high among both the groups. Studies have shown a close link between the level of literacy and the number of child labourers in a State. Studies also indicate that between 85 per cent and 90 per cent of the child labourers in the country are *dalits* and tribals.[9]

Similar statements can be made also about health care. Focus has been on what is known as environmental health i.e. prevention through injections and spraying of pesticides, rather than dealing with the basic issues of hygiene and nutrition. The Scheduled Classes are the ones that need this support the most. Studies indicate that around 40 per cent of the *dalits* and 47 per cent of the tribals are malnourished and that they account for 90 per cent of the families below the poverty line.[10] Even hospital care is not easily accessible to the poor, particularly the Scheduled Classes. The cultural difference between the medical personnel and the urban or rural poor, and the cost involved in going to the health centre and buying medicines, keep the poor away from health care institutions.[11] In other cases, the family with limited financial means takes only boy children to the dispensary. Girl children and the old may be taken there only in case of an extreme need, often when it is too late.[12] Its consequence is seen, among others, in high infant and child mortality among these classes, particularly of girl children.

At the economic level, poverty alleviation programmes are planned but the causes of poverty are not dealt with. Much impoverishment is caused by the pattern of development. For example, studies indicate that there has been massive displacement particularly in the tribal regions. The country does not have a reliable official database on the number and type of displaced people and on the nature of their rehabilitation. An estimate based on secondary sources indicates that at least 213 lakhs have been displaced or otherwise deprived of their livelihood by development projects, between 1951 and 1990. By those norms, their number must have exceeded 300 lakhs by now. At least 40 per cent of them are tribals and another 20 per cent are *dalits*. The proportion of other rural poor is high but we do not have a definite estimate. Fewer than a third of the displaced persons have been resettled even partially.[13] With little or no resettlement, most of those deprived of their livelihood are impoverished and forced to resort to destructive practices such as cutting trees for sale as firewood or filling the urban slums.

Betting on the Strong

Thus the present system ignores the poor and bets on the strong India only has an industrial policy based on productivity and GNP growth, but not a social policy. Unlike the East Asian countries, from a purely economic point of view India did not need to create a class of consumers. Because of its big population, the country could build a whole economy based on the needs of a fast growing middle class. According to estimates, at independence about 10 per cent of a much smaller population belonged to the middle Class. By the 1980s, about 30 per cent of the population or about 200 millions belonged to this class.[14] With such a big middle class, the industrialist did not need to have more consumers. So, unlike in South Korea, India did not need to invest in the health, education, nutrition and hygiene of the poor. It was possible to overcome the guilt feeling through a relief measure of reservations, i.e., making institutions available but not ensuring their access to communities that have been discriminated against for centuries.

Apart from an economic vested interest, India also lacked the social base required to make an investment in this sector. The nature of consciousness depends also on the type of the freedom struggle and the new leadership that emerged from it. In much of East Asia, for example in Indonesia, Korea and China, the new order was achieved through an armed struggle. One of its results is change in the class that assumed power after independence. In India it was peaceful independence. It means that most freedom fighters belonged to the bourgeoisie i.e. the class that produced administrators for the Hindu kings, later joined the Muslim rulers and collaborated with the British. So independence was in fact transfer of power from the foreign ruler to the Indian bourgeoisie.[15] Besides, the freedom movement was funded by the emerging capitalists. To them, it was investment for profit in the future of independent India.[16] This is the class that prepared the Bombay Plan 1945 on which the mixed economy was based. Its basic thinking was that the public sector should build the industrial infrastructure and leave the consumer industry to the public sector. Profit was obviously the motive of what some have called State capitalism.

Besides, the class to which power was transferred at independence, had internalised the colonial ideology. They, therefore, viewed the western form of development as the only one possible. They attributed progress in Europe to technology and did not understand that it was a result of colonialism. European countries had destroyed the economy of the colonies and had de-industrialised them in order to turn them into suppliers of cheap raw material and capital for the Industrial Revolution in the metropolitan country, and into captive markets for its finished products. Because of their ideology, the ruling class of post-independence India viewed national development only in terms of technological progress and GNP growth. They took for granted that some sops to the subalterns in the form of reservations would help them to come up to the standards of the bourgeoisie. But the social system needed no change.[17]

The nature of the ruling class is an important reason why the Indian decision-makers thought only in terms of making the educational, health and other infrastructure available but did not ensure access to the groups that had hitherto been excluded from these services. This class only needed the *dalits* in the Hindu fold as numbers. Social transformation was not their priority as one can see from the Poona Pact.[18] As a result, a small group among the subalterns that could gain access to education despite the obstacles they faced, also got most jobs under the reserved category. That is what the apex court calls the creamy layer. There is a danger of the next generations of this group continuing to get most benefits and excluding the majority from the Scheduled Classes. Thus when reservations are granted without any other social components as in Malaysia, one sees the risk of their becoming a vested interest of the "creamy layer".

In much of East Asia, on the contrary, a different class of rulers emerged as a result of an armed struggle. This class had a social consciousness that was different from the relief and welfare orientation of the bourgeoisie.[19] Though Malaysia attained independence through peaceful means, the independence of Singapore and the ethnic riots of 1969 created the political climate required to build a social base. The Bhumiputra policy emerged from it. The difference between South Asian and East Asian countries can be seen in the fact that the latter spend around 15 per cent of their budget on the social sector,[20] while in India it is around 5 per cent.[21]

Reservations amid Growing Poverty

To this should be added the fact of growing poverty and unemployment. The latter is both among the educated and the unskilled workers. The pattern of development chosen is basic to this situation. Employment generation has to be basic to this approach. It requires labour-creating and capital-saving technology "that takes into consideration the vast potential of human labour and helps the people who are now struggling for survival beyond the fringes of modern technology.[22]

In reality, because of the concentration on sophisticated technology, employment generation has been low. To add to the woes of the poor, mechanisation started with the beginning of the process of liberalisation in the mid-1980s. More jobs were lost as a result. For example, in 1985, the year to which the beginning of the process of liberalisation can be attributed, the formal sector had 30 million employees, in India's total workforce of 310 millions, 23 millions of them in the public sector and 7 millions in the private sector. By 1991, the number in the private sector had come down to 6 millions.[23] Today the total in the formal sector is around 28 millions. With every job in the formal sector lost, several more are lost in the informal sector. According to ILO estimates, 8 million jobs were lost between 1992 and 1994, in a country that requires ten millions new jobs every year.[24]

Reduction in jobs goes hand in hand with consumerism. The multinationals have come to India to make high profits by producing luxury goods for the middle class. The rest of the population does not matter to them. Investment is primarily in luxury goods meant for this middle class. Such consumerism cannot be maintained except by depriving some other group of its basic necessities. The rich countries maintain their lifestyle by over-consuming the resources of the poor countries. In India, the middle class consumerism is at the cost of the poor.[25] Negative employment that we have mentioned as one of its consequences, is of concern to those among the Scheduled Classes that have access to education. With the State withdrawing from the economy and with mechanisation depriving the poor of unskilled jobs, there are very few jobs left even for this category. Of greater importance is the increasing poverty among the Scheduled Classes. Even according to official sources, the proportion of families below the poverty line has grown from 89 per cent in 1989 to 47 per cent in 1992.[26] Obviously most of them are *dalits* and tribals because it is well known that around 90 per cent of these classes live below the poverty line.

Besides, in recent decades a new class of middle caste landowners has become economically and politically powerful. The freedom fighters were on the defensive because of the colonial attacks on their culture. But they also had a feeling of guilt about injustice done to the subaltern castes. The reservations were a result of this feeling of guilt. This newly powerful class of middle caste landowners have got the benefits of the post-independence agricultural policies, as such have also developed a vested interest in the poverty of the subalterns. They are the ones holding many of them in bondage or exploiting them as low paid agricultural labourers. Their access to education and to jobs outside the village is a threat to their power. Moreover, with liberalisation, the social consciousness of the middle class has all but died out. The consumerist middle and commitment to justice cannot go hand in hand. This class has become selfish and opposes measures such as reservations that can bring a semblance of justice to at least a small section among the subalterns.[27]

While the justice dimension became an important issue in East Asia and employment generation went hand in hand with economic growth, in India relatively few jobs were created. They could not keep pace with mass education and a growing population. As a result, only a few from the subaltern classes could join the formal sector to which reservations were limited. These few who could be co-opted into the dominant system, thus cease to represent the class they belong to. In fact, one cannot deny the possibility of the reservations becoming a vested interest of this small group. As unemployment grew, so did competition for a piece of the cake. With rural poverty growing, the opportunities were reduced in the villages. The newly emerging middle castes and those who had held power for centuries began to view those entitled to reservations as a threat.

In reality, a large number of reserved posts had remained unfilled mostly because of high caste prejudices or because *dalit* and tribal lack access to education. These posts were carried over to the next year. This fact was distorted and propaganda made to show that at some stage no job would be available for the middle and high castes. The *dalits*, who were presented as inefficient, would get all the jobs and the efficient high castes would be left out. The fact that these posts were not filled because of the reasons mentioned above, was ignored. Emotions were roused against reservations. The Gujarat riots of 1985, the Mandal agitation of 1990 and other events followed. The apex court passed a judgment on the issue and introduced the concept of the creamy layer.[28]

Searching for Solutions

Amid this din, many persons from the dominant castes demand that the economic criterion should be the only one for reservations. On the other side, many persons from the Scheduled Classes keep insisting that caste/tribe should be the sole criterion. We have seen from the analysis above that neither contention can be accepted in its totality. Having economic criterion alone is bound to go against the Scheduled Classes. With persons from the high castes holding most positions of power in the administration, there is a danger of their diverting most of these benefits to the poor from their own caste.

That is where one has to search for solutions. To begin with, to stop at the reservations, as practised today, can aggravate the danger of what the Supreme Court calls the creamy layer developing a vested interest in it. Most persons from the Scheduled Classes are being further impoverished by the pattern of development. Their marginalisation is being intensified by liberalisation. They are thus deprived of any possibility of freeing themselves from their oppressive state. On the other side, it should be obvious from what has been said above, that a purely economic criterion is bound to go against the Scheduled Classes.

The first conclusion that follows from the above analysis is the reservations are required. Communities that have been discriminated against for centuries, cannot be expected to compete as equals with those who have had access to education and social services for several generations. On the other hand it is difficult to choose between caste and class as the sole criterion for reservations. One can conclude that to be effective, one has to combine caste with class. There is a somewhat strong case to suggest that only those members of the Scheduled Classes below a certain income level should be entitled to reservations. There are also reasons to state that reservations should stop after two or three generations. That improves the possibility of the reservations reaching a bigger number among them.

However, even this measure can only make reservations available to these groups. One has to find ways of ensuring their access to the services like education and health. To ensure it, one has to implement the laws that have been passed but ignored. For example, the country has laws against rural indebtedness, on child labour and bondage. The Constitution speaks of the right to universal primary education. In reality, the State has never enforced any of these rights in the case of the poor. The constitutional rights have been limited to the middle and other politically powerful classes. The educational system itself has not got out of its middle class moorings and can be considered irrelevant to the poor. Unless all these aspects are attended to, social justice will only remain a distant dream.

Conclusion

We have attempted in this chapter an analysis of the situation of reservations in the country. We have cited this very limited measure in the context of the class that led the freedom movement and the pattern of development chosen. Focus has been on building an industrial infrastructure and on making institutions available. A social policy has not been developed. In this context, reservations have become a threat to the classes that have a vested interest in the poverty of the subalterns. Because of this limited vision also, the debate around reservations has been limited to caste or economic factor. The need to make the services available has rarely been discussed.

This issue cannot be understood except in the context of the need to evolve a social policy that the country lacks. In doing it, all the aspects mentioned above have to be attended to. The Malaysian experience as well of that of other East Asian countries has shown that combining availability to these institutions with access to them, can create the social base required to eradicate poverty and enable the poor to join the mainstream as equals, not as cheap labour alone. That is the challenge of the reservation policy.

REFERENCES

1. Bailey, Susan, *Saints, Goddesses and Kings: Muslims and Christians in South Indian Society, 1700-1900.* Cambridge: Cambridge University Press, 1989, pp. 220-221.
2. Sharma, Ursula, "Status Striving and Striving to Abolish Status: The Arya Samaj and the Low Castes," *Social Action,* 26 (n. 3, July-Sept.), 1971, pp. 219-226.
3. Munda, Ram Dayal, "The Jharkhand Movement Retrospect and Prospect", *Social Change*, 18 (n. 2, June), 1988, pp. 29-42.
4. Dass, Bhagwan, "Reservations Today and Tomorrow", in Walter Fernandes (ed). *The Emerging Dalit Identity: The Re-awakening of the Subalterns*, Indian Social Institute, New Delhi, pp. 241-242, 1996.
5. Gueriviere, Paul, "The Choice of Technology: Alternative Technology or

Alternative Society", *Social Action*, 37 (n. 1, Jan.-March), 1987, pp. 70-71.
6. Kurien, C.T., *Our Five Year Plans*. Bangalore: Christian Institute for the Study of Society, 1967.
7. Jetley, Surinder, *Modernising Indian Peasants: A Study of Six Villages in Eastern Uttar Pradesh*. New Delhi: Asian Educational Services, 1977, p. 56.
8. Naik, J.P., *Equality, Quality and Quantity: The Elusive Triangle of Indian Education*, Allied Publishers, New Delhi, 1975.
9. Fernandes, Walter, Neera Burra and Tara Anand, *Child Labour in India: Poverty, Exploitation and Vested Interests*. New Delhi: Indian Social Institute (mimeo), 1986.
10. Singh, Amar Kumar, "Tribal Attitudes to the Tribals and Non-Tribals in South Bihar", in Amar Kumar Singh and M.K. Jabbi (eds.), *Tribals in India: Development, Deprivation and Discontent*, Council for Social Development, New Delhi, 1995, pp. 294-332.
11. De Souza, Alfred, *The Social Organisation of Aging among the Urban Poor*. New Delhi: Indian Social Institute, 1980.
12. Chen, Lincoln, C. Emadul Huq and Stan D'Souza, "Sex Bias in the Allocation of Food and Health Care in Rural Bangladesh", *Population and Development Review*, 7 (n. 1, March), 1981.
13. Fernandes, Walter, "Development-Induced Displacement in Eastern India", in S.C. Dube (ed.), *Antiquity and Modernity in Tribal India: Vol. I: Continuity and Change among Indian Tribals*. Inter-India Publications, New Delhi, 1998
14. Desrochers, John, "Guidelines for the Anti-Poverty Struggle", *Integral Liberation* 1 (n. 3, Sept.), 1997, pp. 197-223.
15. Sarkar, Sumit, *Modern India 1887-1947*, Macmillan, New Delhi, 1983.
16. Shankardass, Rani Dhavan, *The First Congress Raj*. Macmillan India, New Delhi, 1982.
17. Fernandes, Walter and Arundhuti Roy Choudhury, "Mercantile Colonialism: Destruction of the Economy and Subservience", Paper Presented at the *International Conference Colonialism to Globalisation: Five Centuries After Vasco-da-Gama*; New Delhi: Indian Social Institute, February 2-5, 1998.
18. *Ibid.*
19. Coronel-Ferrer, Miriam, "The Specificity of the Freedom Struggle and Leadership in Southeast Asia", Paper Presented at the *International Conference Colonialism to Globalisation: Five Centuries After Vasco da Gama*, New Delhi: Indian Social Institute, February 2-6, 1998.
20. Jomo, K.S., "Emulating Southeast Asian Development: The Neo-Liberal Tale of Two Studies", Paper Presented at the *International Conference Colonialism to Globalisation: Five Centuries After Vasco-da-Gama*, New Delhi: Indian Social Institute, February 2-6, 1998.
21. Govt. of India, *Economic Survey 1997-98*, New Delhi: Government of India, 1998.

22. Solomon, Bhakter R., "Appropriate Technology: An Indian Point of View", *Reading Rural Development Communication Bulletin* (n. 9, March), 1980.
23. Patnaik, Gopabandhu and Damodar Panda, "The New Economic Policy and the Poor", *Social Action* 42 (n. 2, April-June), 1992, pp. 206-207.
24. VAK, "The New Economic Path: Trends and Impact," *Globalisation and SAP: Trends and Impact.* Mumbai: edited by Ajit Muriken, Vikas Adhyayan Kendra, Mumbai, 1997.
25. *Ibid.*
26. *Ibid.*
27. Kothari, Rajni, "State and Statelessness in Our Times", *Economic and Political Weekly*, 26 (11 & 12, Annual Number), 1991, pp. 553-558.
28. *Ibid.*

2

RETHINKING SCHEDULED CASTE RESERVATION

SACHCHIDANANDA

Never before has a democratic nation embarked on such a profound reordering of its social structure as India after the attainment of independence. The new Constitution abolished untouchability, a practice rooted in the social life of India for thousands of years. The Fundamental Rights contain the ban on discrimination on grounds of religion, caste, sex, language, etc. Equal treatment for all people was secured. But it was recognized that equality will not overcome the cumulative disadvantages of those at the bottom of the social hierarchy. To promote the advancement of scheduled castes, scheduled tribes and other backward groups the Constitution allowed protective or compensatory discrimination. This was a deliberate departure from the formal forms of equality in order to offset the historic inequalities of these groups.

Reservations are of three types. There are reservations which facilitate access to valid positions and resources. The most important instances of this type are reserved seats in legislatures, reservation of posts in government services and reservation of places in technical and professional colleges. The reservations in legislatures were provided for ten years only initially. But they have been continued through renewals every ten years. Reservation in government posts in many parts of India for some groups in the backward classes is a legacy of the British period. It has now been expanded. The same is the case with reservations in educational institutions. This indeed is necessary to get adequate numbers of qualified people for filling the posts reserved for them in various kinds of government services.

II

Reservation has been regarded by some authorities as a pernicious doctrine. It originated as a remedy for sins of the past of a social order which we have deliberately sought to obliterate. The present generation is, in the process, punished for the actions of their ancestors. It is also held that there is no end to this process. Originally designed only for the scheduled castes and tribes it has been gradually extended to the other backward classes. There is increasing pressure for providing reservations for women, the minorities and the disabled. Compensatory discrimination has become India's new *mantra* for each and every caste clamouring for removal of backwardness. It has brought India to a state of compensatory backwardness.

The theory of compensatory discrimination is built around compensation for past social inequities. However, the remedies for removal of social inequalities lie not in political or legal action but in changing the social structure. People who seek political remedies for social injustices do not solve the problem. Proponents of social justice argue that empowering the poor and the backward will automatically solve the problem, but experience has shown that it is not so.

The entire strategy of reservations has been hailed by Galanter as a 'costly success'. There is no doubt that it has produced considerable redistributive effects. Reserved seats in legislative bodies increase the flow of patronage, attention and favourable policy to scheduled castes. The provisions of jobs has given them steady income, security, information, patronage and prestige. So far as caste reservations in educational institutions are concerned, there has been enormous wastage of resources but there has also been a major redistribution of educational opportunities. However such redistribution is not spread evenly throughout the beneficiary groups. The benefits have been cornered by a cluster of certain kin groups. This is on account of certain structural factors. The better situated among the beneficiaries enjoy a disproportionate share of programme benefits. Compensatory programmes provide the basis for personal achievements and enlarge the beneficiaries' capacities to share their own lives. The promise of good positions offers a powerful incentive for individual efforts.

Reservations in legislatures have helped the scheduled castes to enter them and influence policy affecting the *dalits* even if only to a limited extent. It opened out the political world to the *dalits* who had been earlier denied access. Without reservation it would not have been possible for them to get elected. In the Eighth Lok Sabha even after 30 years of independence only two scheduled caste candidates were elected from non-reserved seats. It has also led to the emergence of professional politicians among the scheduled castes.

They have to strike a balance between obtaining the support of scheduled castes and gaining acceptance from the electorate as a whole. This results in a role conflict. A close identification with the *dalit* cause may result in alienating the large caste Hindu population. Once he is assured of their support, he does not bother about the support of his own people. Thus they abdicate the responsibility to their people.

Parvathamma has shown that a few families in each State corner the bulk of the reserved seats. The same person is elected for five or six consecutive terms. Such people enjoy the fruit of political reservations quite independent of possible obligations. The gap between the legislators and their constituents in terms of education, occupation, wealth and urban/rural background is considerable. The bulk of the scheduled caste members in the third, fourth and fifth Lok Sabhas were drawn from a tiny proportion (0.3 per cent) of educated scheduled castes. Although 72 per cent of the scheduled castes are agricultural workers only 36 per cent are drawn from their category. 9.2 per cent were drawn from trade and commerce in which a very small percentage of scheduled castes are engaged. Urban-based professionals, lawyers, doctors, and educationists have a higher representation. Evidence from the States like Andhra Pradesh, Maharashtra and Uttar Pradesh leads to the same conclusion. It reveals the consolidation of the hegemonic rules of a few amongst the scheduled castes.

The existence of a sizeable number of scheduled caste legislators has not made any difference to the acute poverty, degraded living conditions and caste violence experienced by the *dalits*. On account of party affiliation, the S.C. legislators have failed to evolve an effective networking amongst themselves to act as a united pressure group to work on an agreed minimum programme of action. They are mainly concerned with the implementation of reservations in education and employment. They have been unable to secure the effective implementation of the welfare and development schemes for the scheduled castes. The existing political system has succeeded in reducing them to the position of puppets in the hands of dominant political elite. It is difficult to disagree with Dushkin's observation that protective discrimination as a whole has become a mechanism of social control, an instrument of distributionist policies. The politics of caste has successfully divided the ranks of the poor along lines of caste divisions and prevented their coming together on a class basis.

Reservation for political positions has reduced the monopoly of political power of the traditionally dominant groups. Emergent leaders belonging to non-schedule categories see their future doomed if they hail from reserved constituencies. They, therefore, resent reservations. Reservation in government employment has made it possible for a large number of scheduled castes to occupy their position. Without reservation they could not have qualified. People who have made to the government service have formed a middle class, maintain a distance from their castemen and imitate the life-style and values of the middle class. There has been fifteen times increase in the number of scheduled castes going in for post-matric education. This has resulted in growing unemployment among the scheduled caste youths. Economic differentiation among the deprived communities has become sharp. The privileged strata among them has not yet been incorporated in the general middle class. To some extent reservations have slowed down the growth of militancy among the deprived groups.

III

Protective discrimination has belied the hopes of its protagonists. Even Ambedkar conceived of it as a temporary self-liquidating device. It was hoped that the reservation would soon bridge the gap between the deprived groups and others. However, it was not realised that the non-reserved groups would also develop and at a much faster rate than the scheduled castes and as such, the distance between the two would continue. No minimum standard in regard to education and employment was prescribed for any group before it could be descheduled. It is clear that occupation, ignorance, illiteracy and poverty levels have not been fixed.

It is, however, necessary to look at the parameters of backwardness in a dynamic perspective. Scheduled Castes are no longer as uniformly backward as when they were scheduled. Both caste groups and individuals within them have moved up and reached a point at which they seem to be less deserving of preferential treatment. In some instances, the entire caste groups have advanced in terms of education and employment and have shed completely the disabilities from which they were suffering. Some communities like the Mahars of Maharashtra, Chamars of Western Uttar Pradesh and Gujarat are today much better off than some of the castes that were not considered to be backward enough to be included in the schedule. This causes strong resentment and leads to caste riots in some parts of India. Added to this, is the fact that the advance among different scheduled castes has been uneven. The castes that have failed to use the facilities continue to be backward because they are not in a position to reach out to the support offered.

The only solution to do away with these anomalies would be to deschedule individuals or castes that have advanced. Article 342 clearly specifies a procedure for this purpose. The Government of India appointed the Lokur Committee to go into this problem. It recommended the rescheduling of 14 tribes and 28 castes. The Chamars of Uttar Pradesh, Bihar and Punjab and the Mahars of Maharashtra were among the castes recommended for descheduling. The scheduled caste leadership was extremely hostile to this report. As such, it was not accepted by the government. Subsequent effort to revise the list ended in additions rather than deletions. Thus protective discrimination became a system of entry without an exit. The operation of reservations in legislatures has been extended every ten years. It has come to be self-perpetuating. Since the scheduled castes form about one-seventh of the total population, none of the political parties would be prepared to take the risk of alienating this vote bank. Thus the reservation issue has been politicised. It is no longer a device for raising the quality of life of the scheduled castes. The only way out is to lay down a minimum level of development together with doing away with disabilities in respect of caste as well as individuals. As far as the individuals are concerned the top achievers among the scheduled castes do not suffer from caste disabilities. In each caste there is a creamy layer which can do without reservation. The Chinappa Reddy Report in Andhra Pradesh has laid down detailed criteria for this purpose. It may be adopted on an all-India level. This would considerably reduce resentment against reservation prevalent in the general population. It may be noted that the compensatory programmes affect the morale and initiative of those they want to help. However, the people who clamour for the continuance of reservations are those who do not need them most. As a matter of fact those who need it most do not have access to it.

IV

Any discourse on the issue of reservation must explore other avenues of reducing and ultimately removing the backwardness of the scheduled castes. The entire issue is tied up with the socio-economic development of the society and change in the social structure itself. It must also be seen in the context of population growth which is outstripping job opportunities. It continues the increasing burden on a developing society with large numbers at or below the poverty line. Since social status moves in consonance with economic opportunities, placement in the job market and acquisition of skills to be upwardly mobile are very important. It is, therefore, equally necessary to see that the basic task is that of enlarging the cake, widening opportunities for education and employment and controlling population growth. It would be better to pay more attention to the education of the scheduled castes, to improve their skills so as to give them better employment opportunities. They should be prepared to be able to compete with others and claim an equal share in an achieving society in which the economic cake grows more rapidly. Levelling up is a better answer than levelling down. All efforts must be made to make the reservations really effective so that its need fades away.

One significant attempt in this direction has been made by a voluntary organisation, the Sulabh International under the leadership of Dr. Bindeshwar Pathak. It grew out of the Bhangi Mukti Movement initiated during the Gandhi Centenary Year, 1969. Its aim is to liberate the Bhangi or the Valmiki who is at the bottom of the scheduled caste hierarchy as his occupation was disposal of human waste. Since it was a highly polluting occupation their social status was not only the lowest but their style of life was demeaning and sub-human. Dr. Pathak devised a method of replacing dry latrines by pour flush privies at a low cost so that there was no need for their services. Thus a large number of Valmikis were liberated. But this was not enough. They had to be given alternative employment. For their rehabilitation various kinds of training programmes were initiated. These included carpentry, electric wiring, cycle repairing, tailoring, motor driving etc. Good schools were established for their children. Armed with good education and skills in various trades, they learnt dignity of labour and had a high moral. Valmikis were also given social prestige by various methods. Thus through social, economic and psychological measures, the Valmikis were brought in the mainstream of national life without any confrontation with any section of society. They have gained confidence, enjoy a better quality of life and have been empowered to stand on their own feet without the need for any preferential treatment.

Thus looking for political and legal remedies for social injustices will not suffice. Backwardness and poverty can only be eradicated through societal change. The challenge is not only to the State but to

Indian society. Indian social system has shown the strength, the capacity and stability to face many a challenge. One way to achieve this is fast transition to modern technology and through efforts to achieve national integration. Unity in diversity is India's civilizational strength. An outward looking vision will provide exposure of the people to new technologies, new ideas, newer types of organizations and other means to bring about the desired societal change. Reservation means distributing limited jobs and economic opportunities. There is need to create more jobs, more educational opportunities, accelerate economic growth and create more income.

The entire issue has also to be seen in the human rights perspective like the question of bonded labour, child labour etc. Equality of social and economic opportunities should be provided for all at the ground level. There is an urgent need for bringing the more deprived groups among the scheduled castes in the development net. It is seen that with the extension of reservations for the other backward castes, the stress on making reservation effective for the scheduled castes has been diluted. It is imperative that a national consensus should be evolved on this issue irrespective of the political compulsions. The process could be facilitated by clearly defining the elements of backwardness of the scheduled castes so that reservations are not reduced to mechanical administrative measures rather than carefully designed strategies for the advance of the most disadvantaged section of Indian society.

NOTES

Abbasayulu, V.V., 1980, *Emergence of Political Leadership in Scheduled Castes: A Sociological Study of Scheduled Caste Legislators in Andhra Pradesh*, Centre for Harijan Studies, Osmania University, Hyderabad.

Chitnis, S., 1997, *Definition of Terms Scheduled Castes and Scheduled Tribes: A Case of Ambivalence Politics of Backwardness* (Ed.) by V.A. Pai Panandikar, Konark Publishers Pvt. Ltd., Delhi.

Deshpande, N., 1970, *Towards Social Integration: Problem of Adjustment of Scheduled Caste Elite in India*, Delhi.

Dushkin, L., 1972, *Scheduled Caste Politics in Mahar* (Ed.) The Untouchables in Contemporary India, University of Arizona Press, Tuscon.

Galanter, M. 1984, *Competing Equalities*, Oxford University Press, Delhi.

Lynch, O.M., 1969, *The Politics of Untouchability: Society, Mobility and Social Change in a City of India*, Columbia University Press, New York.

Parvathamma, C., 1990, *The Clamour for Reservation*, Institute for Development Studies, Madras.

Sachchidananda, 1977, *The Harijan Elite*, Thomson Press, Faridabad.

Sachchidananda, 1997, Reservations and After: The case of Bihar in V.A. Pai Panandikar (Ed.), *The Politic of Backwardness*, Konark Publishers Pvt. Ltd., Delhi

Shah, G., 1990, *Reservations, Promise and Performance*, Institute of Development Studies, Madras.

3

SOCIAL INTERVENTION FOR SOCIAL JUSTICE

R.R. SINGH

> *"It is easier to change situation than behaviour;*
> *it is easier to change behaviour than attitude, and*
> *it is easier to change attitude than value."*

Introduction

An attempt is made in this chapter to explore the substantive and processual aspects of protective discrimination with special reference to the scheduled castes. Although protective discrimination in the constitutional design covers scheduled castes, scheduled tribes and other backward classes, it will become too broad an area to be dealt with in this short chapter, references to the scheduled tribes would be made only at places. Further stress will be laid on education and economic upgradation of the scheduled castes in the present discussion than other aspects. It may also be noted at the outset that with the emergence of coalition politics at different levels and announcements of common minimum programmes, national agendas and their likes, the life-span of development plans is bound to be short-lived. Plans will be re-oriented or re-formulated. This is bound to adversely affect the process of social development.

Constitutional Mandate

Several articles of the Constitution relate to social justice and equality, and, read in their totality, strengthen the provision for protective discrimination. Some of them, which are most relevant to the present discussion, are: equality before law (Art. 14), prohibition of discrimination (Art. 15), equality of opportunity in matters of public employment (Art. 16), abolition of untouchability (Art. 17), protection of life and personal liberty (Art. 21), prohibition of forced labour (Art. 23), establishment of a social order and promotion of welfare of people (Art. 38), equitable distribution of material resources and protection of weaker sections (Art. 39), equal justice and free legal aid (Art. 39A), promotion of economic and educational interests of scheduled castes, scheduled tribes and other weaker sections (Art. 46), upholding unity [Art. 51-A(c)], rendering national service [Art. 51-A(d)], Promoting harmony among all people [Art. 51-A(e)], and also Articles 330, 332, 335 and 338.

As Marc Galanter has put it, some of these articles which make special provisions in favour of a class of citizens suffering from cumulative nature of group inequalities come under the category of affirmative action. They have been designed to deal with "competing inequalities" in a "compartmental society". They are mediatory mechanisms to deal with tensions which arise between individual and group needs (or rights), hierarchy and equality, and social policy and social reality. Compensatory or positively discriminatory provisions thus are concerned with the historical restitution or reparation and thereby deliverance of social justice to the socially disadvantaged groups. The caste system in India has been described by Ken Cooper as more degrading than slavery in the United States. He has also reported his interview with a group of youth in Kerala who do not feel discriminated against. The situation in the northern part of India however is quite different.

Need for Social Intervention

The above-mentioned general and special provisions of the Constitution and other judicial and executive actions fall under the definition of social intervention for social justice. They seek to change the perceptions of citizens about themselves and other social groups or vice versa: change the attitudes and behaviour patterns of individuals and groups, and also change their material situation. The persistence of social need and social distance is therefore an area for continuing social action, Since this, in turn, is bound to generate conflict, conflict-resolution too becomes one of the major goals for securing social justice.

Suma Chitnis has brought out clearly the situation of scheduled caste students in the Indian Institute of Technology. There are those who leave voluntarily; those who are asked to discontinue; or who are transferred to other institutions, and also the span period of those who complete the course. It has also been found that drop-out rate in educational institutions is more from among those families or households which are below the poverty line. Admissions in the IITs in quite a few cases have created problems at several levels because the students from the general and reserved categories do not start from a level playing field. These generate frustrations and resentments between the two groups of students, between students and the faculty, and even between the creamy layer and other students belonging to the reserved categories. When the students fail to compete in professional and technical courses, they either change their stream or join the non-formal system. In either case, it leads to inferiorization which defeats the very enabling provisions of the Constitution. It creates a new kind of psychological disability. While suggestions for remedial courses at a very early stage and neighbourhood schools have been made they are yet to take roots. This only shows that the achievement of interrelated goals of social justice, equality and excellence require painstaking and continuing efforts in order to reduce the number of the historically socially disadvantaged groups and thereby release resources for development in general and also for the newly emerging groups suffering from social, economic or developmental disadvantages or relapses in particular. In the field of education, the remedial learning programme of the Homi Bhabha Centre for Science Education in Jalgaon district of Maharashtra is an example of sensitivity and responsiveness required to address to the needs of the socially under-privileged groups. In the Sulabh Public School, although girls are being educated to resist gender bias, Balmiki and other pupils share common facilities, boys and girls emulate good role models and the problem of drop-out is virtually non-existent; certain remedial measures have still been suggested in a comprehensive evaluation report in order to neutralize the effects and disadvantages of early socialization. These only prove that equality of opportunity without compensatory and continuing inputs will not result in the equality of outcome. Sustained educational, cultural, development and social action are needed in order to offset historical and newer disadvantages for equipping the concerned groups to face the challenges of modernization, globalization and post-industrial society. The cumulative nature of disadvantages reflect themselves in psychological, social, cultural, economic, institutional, locational and developmental domain. Interventions however are not adequately addressing to the psycho-social and cultural aspects adequately which will be clear from the State's response to the problem of social inequality given below.

State Support to Protective Discrimination

The Annual Report of the Ministry of Welfare, Government of India (1996-97) brings out that three-fourths of the scheduled castes are engaged in primary occupations. The average literacy rate in this group is low (37 per cent) and the drop-out rate is high. The *Dalit* Manifesto brought out by social activists (National Action Forum for Social Justice) had been incorporated in the Common Minimum Programme (CMP) of the former United Front Government. The Forum had suggested Special/Mobile Courts, and population equivalent proportion of the total plan provision of the Centre and States for scheduled castes to meet the ends of social justice. Protection of Civil Rights Act (1955), Prevention of Atrocities against Scheduled Castes and Scheduled Tribes Act (1989), National Scheduled Castes and Scheduled Tribes Finance and Development Corporation, National Scheme for the Liberation and Rehabilitation of Scavengers, Special Component Plan, Special Central Assistance, National Commission for Safai Karamcharis and individual or household based criteria for eligibility are instruments to achieve the goal of social justice. Ten per cent of special assistance, among others, is earmarked for vulnerable groups, 40 per cent for the scheduled castes and 25 per cent for those below the poverty line. Problems such as shortfalls in the utilization of grants or diversions of allocations by the States too have been reported. The response of the State mainly falls in the domain of welfare (i.e., admission to educational institutions, protection (i.e., abolition of untouchability), and development (i.e., grant or subsidy for housing or drinking water well). While the manifestation of historical social disadvantage is showing gradual change, continuing atrocities against these groups are a matter of grave concern. They are indicators of persisting social exclusion and inadequate societal response thereto.

Lessons from Urban Studies

A study conducted by the Delhi School of Social Work on scavengers in Delhi (1997) and another on Scheduled Castes in Delhi (1996) furnish data about the size of the family, monthly income, monthly expenditure on food, poor savings, reliance by majority of the respondents on noninstitutional sources for borrowing, and almost all the scavengers requiring financial assistance. These show the enormity of their social need. Most of these groups are migrants, illiterate, and live in slums, resettlement colonies and *jhuggi-jhopri* clusters. Those who are particularly associated with the degrading occupation of scavenging do receive some benefits in kind, and they also occasionally take up petty jobs to supplement family income. It is very difficult to estimate the monetary value of these supplementary earnings. Moreover, if it is known that certain social benefits will be available at a specified income threshold, the prospective beneficiaries tend to give information on individual and household income accordingly in order to ensure their eligibility for a particular programme. Studies on the impact of integrated rural development, poverty alleviation and welfare in India and abroad have shown such trends. Cases are known of "splits" or "divisions" in the families in order to claim double or multiple benefits. In this occupational group, as in other poverty groups, persistence of poverty is related not only to income but also to consumption and capability. The latter has been brought out clearly in the human development reports published by the United Nations Development Programme.

The question arises about the method of prioritization in view of the limited resources. For example, when 94 per cent of the respondents have got income below Rs. 2000 per month and average size of their families is six, the question arises as to who should be selected? for what quantum of assistance? and how? If a family has got an alcoholic or a substance abuser, a person with disability, an infirm elderly, chronically ill person, an abusive head of the household, non-school going or drop-out children, a history of saving or debt, or record of crime or deviance, such a family is certainly in need of assistance.

Such a need, however, can be met through humanitarian and welfare measures. A financial institution would not accept these criteria for sanctioning loan or subsidy unless a family's or individual's record gives an indication of their capability and viability. Secondly, sanction of loan is not a sufficient condition for its utilization. What is needed is regular social guidance, individualized assistance and monitoring to ensure that funds are properly utilized and the economic status of the household shows upgradation. This aspect, therefore, deserves serious consideration if the scarce resources are to be targeted properly. The need, therefore, is to develop differential indicators for determining the eligibility of households for providing welfare assistance so that families are able to meet their subsistence needs; and economic assistance to them (loans or subsidies) for promoting entrepreneurship. How far below a household is above or below the poverty line (or double the poverty line) will determine the depth or otherwise of poverty and, therefore, the threshold of eligibility for one or the other form of intervention. Reported income alone will not serve as a sufficient indicator of need or eligibility unless other factors too are taken into account. This calls for a sensitive and differential approach to the identification of need and its fulfilment through economic and social intervention than a standard bureaucratic approach. The former will be based on a continue of opportunity, access, process (input) and outcome. While prioritization of individual and household needs will help in evolving effective need-meeting strategies, its increasing politicization would prove to be an impediment. This aspect however is being ignored, and the spate of populist programmes are largely resulting in the misutilization of resources.

The Phenomenon of Inclusionary-Exclusion

Application of the provisions of equality and affirmative action in the Constitution has definitely made a difference in the last fifty years. However, the emergence of a phenomenon, which may be called inclusionary-exclusion, deserves serious attention. This means that facilities provided in educational institutions, reservations in jobs, and house sites etc. meant to bring the socially disadvantaged groups on par with other groups, are yet to achieve the goal of social integration, for, these groups are yet to overcome the feelings of inferiority, segregation and exclusion. It further means that the system formally includes the underprivileged groups and assumes that integration is taking place, whereas in reality processes of psycho-social exclusion continue to work to the detriment of the scheduled castes and scheduled tribes. In order to materialize them, the initiative of the Tata Institute of Social Sciences to help such disadvantaged groups is noteworthy. Inclusion is therefore at the physical and material levels. Psycho-social exclusion persists. Such disadvantaged students in the educational institutions adopt the life-styles of their counterparts, and thus virtually overcompensate to the detriment of their studies in order to show that they too are like them. They also reject special coaching of this reason. This phenomenon can be dealt with by the civil society more effectively than the State institutions, populist programmes, or politicization of disadvantaged groups. The concept of capability poverty introduced in the Human Development Reports of the UNDP, which included income, health and literacy, and the concept of exit time requires to be further expanded and refined to include the process and the degree of system-generated inferiorization and extent of social exclusion. Quite a few students do not avail compensatory or remedial programmes because they will prove to be socially stigmatizing.

Needed Social Intervention

In order to deal with the above problems, early childhood intervention head-start programmes, additional psycho-social inputs in educational institutions for effective liaisoning between teachers, parents and students etc. are needed. Behavioural change will come through social participation more than the acquisition of knowledge and skills only which are stressed at present. Individualization and socialization need to go together. Although education itself is a socializer, educational socialization will require to be consciously attempted. Rural-urban differentials in the social sector are well-known and the latter provide the locational advantage to all over the others. Social disadvantage, combined with that of locational and institutional, obstruct the compensatory provisions and the mechanisms. Added to these is the growing caste consciousness, and social distances assuming the form of social divides due to rising aspirations for a better life, frustration and politicization. In this connection, the observations and anguish of the former Lok Sabha Speaker P. Sangma about requests for recommendation letters from the students belonging to the scheduled tribes from the north-eastern States at 40 per cent level performance assume importance. While the State can initiate affirmative action programmes, it is the society which has to sustain it. It may be noted that among the three dimensions of justice in the Constitution, social precedes economic and political, and it is difficult to come by. Social justice therefore calls for social intervention, for, it cannot be achieved by State action alone through law or uniform schemes.

In order to correct the dysfunctionality of a stratified traditional society, the Constitution has enjoined upon the State and its citizens to work for the creation of not only a just but socially just society. While the response of citizens to achieve this goal has been feeble, the State, to use the phrase of Upendra Baxi, too has preferred to promote, as it happens, the justice of power over the power of justice. The game of numbers has polarized social groups, fuelled social strife, and tensions, delayed the formulation of development plans and their implementation through re-allocations, diversions and non-utilization of resources; has led to a series of populist announcements with resultant frustrations and growing fractured polity, eroded the credibility of political leadership of institutions due to unseemly sights in legislatures and Parliament. Arrogation in politics has resulted in the derogation of culture, and relegation of substantive programmes of social justice. Thus politics comes prior to people seems to overrun. Social justice is being used as a slogan to perpetuate the justice of power in a growing environment of social insecurity. Development has come to mean distribution of grants, loans and subsidies to win votes. In such a situation, the institutions of civil society need to forge alliances and create proper ambience for securing social citizenship for all. Growing irrelevance of political parties, opportunistic alliances and non-alliances and rising mortality rates of political parties and governments in spite of expansive ministries are indicators of the inadequacy of politics as an instrument of social justice for citizens in general and socially disadvantaged groups in particular. Excessive politicization of issues has resulted in the emergence of a political society. A process of social inversion seems to be taking place where politics is overriding people, and the latter are being used as carriers of political burden by paying for premature elections and choosing representatives who increasingly fail to represent them for a full term. The rising cases of fake voting, repeat polling, booth capturing and now a new phenomenon of village capturing are pointers to the perpetuation of political injustice, and they relegate to the background the question of social injustice. The end of perpetuating power has overtaken the means through which political justice should be dispensed with. If this is the state of polity, the economy is not far behind. Both were supposed to work in tandem with progressive social groups and forces in society to bring about social change. Now new forms of "kinships" are emerging which do not auger well for the society. This is why social intervention is constituents of the Constitution, namely the executive, the judiciary, the legislature and the people (citizens), it is the latter which has been ignored hitherto.

NOTES

Delhi School of Social Work. Two Studies: One on Scheduled Castes and the other on Scavengers (1996 & 1998).

Education for Equity: Comprehensive Evaluation Sulabh Public School, New Delhi (n.d.)

Galanter, Marc, *Competing Equalities,* Delhi, Oxford Publishing Co., 1984.

Hebsur, R. K., (ed.), *Social Intervention for Justice,* Bombay: Tata Institute of Social Sciences, 1996.
Ministry of Welfare, Government of India, *Annual Report – 1996-97.*
National Action Forum of Social Justice, Dalit Manifesto (1986).
Span (September-October 1997).
Tata Institute of Social Science, *Annual Report, 1995-96* Mumbai.
UNDP, *The Human Development Report, 1997.*

4

PROTECTIVE DISCRIMINATION
Social Necessity or Political Compulsion?

A. K. LAL

Protective discrimination is a constitutional obligation that seeks to compensate people unfavourably located in scheme of resource endowment for the loss incurred on account of their exploitation and stagnation. It seeks to right past wrong as it is wedded to the task of reducing the weight of the past to facilitate appropriation of the benefits of the present. It is intended to provide redress to wounds of disability and disadvantages through their protection and upliftment. Oppressed and exploited are to be compensated through special considerations oriented to right past negative effect. It aspires to graduate the disabled and disadvantaged at the bottom of the stratification system from "their present state of penury to any livable standard or from social bondage to a state of full citizenship.[1] Such initiatives are oriented to elimination of constraints of inherited inferiority and are facilitative to the fostering of norms of a civil society. Consistently exploited and persistently oppressed deserve succour to get themselves out of a situation of cumulative inequality. This in turn requires removal of the initial resource constraints. Underprivileged are to be supported to ensure equality even if it amounts to depriving the privileged. Comprising special dispensations it is oriented to ensure their complete involvement in the emerging opportunity structure. Such provisions seek to enable the lowest and dispossessed to acquire needed skills and orientations for survival. Its intents are thus integrative as it opposes culture of exclusion. It is a means of recompensing people for being kept deprived and segregated. Past experiences of discrimination as well as constraints of protective segregation need to be removed through group-based reparations. Protective discrimination is an impressive strategy to compensate for past privations and a way of neutralizing the present competitive disadvantage to ensure equality of opportunity to the segregated and excluded. It is thus "at once a collective expression of regret, a long-overdue gesture of historical reconciliation, a form of loyalty and an attempt to take the moral sting out of the past as well as to leave the succeeding generation a better society"[2] Principle of systematic preference in favour of historically deprived group led to formulations of policies favouring reservation in educational institutions, bureaucracy and legislative bodies. It comprises series of ameliorative programmes and preferential schemes to favour the weaker sections of the society.

Preferences thus include reservations, to facilitate access to valued resources and positions, programmes involving expenditure or provision of services and special protections.[3] Measures initiated under the policy constitute State intervention seeking promotion of equality in context of traditionally legitimised exploitation. It seems to have found favour as one of the strategies of the "larger social animations penetrating the national freedom movement" and represents a denial of the Darwinian ideology.[4] It marks a shift in earlier commitment to merit and professional competence as bases of public recruitment.

Initially in its comprehensive form it was primarily oriented to help the scheduled communities. Segregation in the case of untouchables and isolation in the case of tribals created a situation of structural disadvantage conducive to perpetuation of their exploitation. Placed at the base of the stratification system the untouchables were condemned to live in poverty, ignorance and inferiority. The situation of cumulative disadvantage led to their segregation and suppression. Similarly, exteriority and insularity imposed low level of material existence in the case of the tribals. Their collective deprivation is attributed to their distinct culture and isolated inhabitation. To such section of the society preferences were made available on communal basis without regard to income and social standing of individual beneficiaries. Protective discrimination in favour of these people therefore constitutes a landmark in India's pursuit of equality and is "an intriguing instance of using law to reshape recalcitrant social patterns."[5] It has a long past. Used initially to facilitate provisions for stipends in elementary schools, reservation to backward classes constituted theme of inquiry commissions, and policy contents for implementation in colonial India also. Limitations notwithstanding such intents represent a safe and predictable road to social mobility for a segment of society denied access to the elementary necessities of life. It seems to have profoundly affected the course of change among these communities. It has helped cause a major breakthrough in amelioration of the condition of the deprived communities. Significant strides have been made in laying the infrastructure to sponsor upward mobility of the historically disadvantaged through the policy of protective discrimination. Significant strides favouring the initiative are evident in their representation at different levels of status and skills. It seems to have marked inauguration of a better future for them. In fact the "coming up of the exploited people from the lowest estate into which any people have ever fallen anywhere at any time in human history has been feasible through preferment both in education and job."[6]

Notwithstanding its achievements, it seems to have caused differentiation among the erstwhile homogeneous communities. Such sections as are more developed than others appear more poised not only to avail new opportunities in education, bureaucracy and politics but are also primary recipients of target-specific State interventions. The weakest in spite of being deserving remain untouched from the benefits as it remains stuck up at the top in the intra-community hierarchy. Poor sections among the excluded communities find themselves twice deprived. Thus it tends to be lopsided in its effect as it has led to development at upper end and stagnation at the bottom.[7] In its impact the compensatory principle tends to decrease the inequalities between the individual members of each caste and community.[8] Classification is said to be the essence of discrimination.

Politics of protection seems to have ensured limited power to elites from the deprived communities as they are constrained to operate at the margin of the power structure. Such elites constitute the periphery unable to penetrate inward to the centre on account of excessive dependencies and little control over the scarce resources. Political acceptance of the leaders is determined also by intra-segmental cleavages. Bases of inequalities especially their institutional mechanism to facilitate are moreoftenthannot found to be beyond comprehension of such leadership. Their zeal to faithfully articulate the needs of their constituents has been found to be inadequate. In spite of its operation the *dalits* are still unfavourably placed in the purity-defilement scale, as they remain exterior. Caste-enforced restrictions persist, as ritual-neutrality tends to be extra-domestic. Caste identities tend to have hardened within the cleavages embedded. Simultaneous operation of traditional as well as modern system of stratification has led the emergence of a situation of status inconsistency in their case. Their divergent location in multiple systems of stratification tends to be a perpetual source of stress to them. Such provisions provoke the ire and envy of those having unchallenged control over the resources of prosperity and dominance as they consider such half-men of exiguous moral resources to be illegitimate competitors for much prized white-collar and professional positions. Leaders from these sections are also criticized for their reconciliatory orientation in politics. The radicals in the left find the policy inimical to the mobilisation of the proletariat on the class lines. It tends to be evasive to the immediate and fundamental problems of the scheduled communities.[9] It has operated as an 'efficient and inexpensive mechanism for social control.[10] The policy has been criticised for its role in making the well meaning caste Hindus indifferent to the plight of *dalits*. It is an opiate which has put the conscience of the upper classes and upper castes to sleep.[11] Gandhian approach to private voluntarism stands supplanted in the wake of existence of State-supported protective discrimination. It has "inhibited a new Mahatma decrying passionately against remaining injustices and the development of an untouchable leader capable of building a movement outside the walls of government privileges and patronage".[12] These weaknesses do not make a case for the discontinuation of the policy of protective discrimination. Its continuation needs to be stressed to enable them find location in power structure. This in turn is needed to ensure the availability of existing facilities favouring upward mobility of the larger sections in the community. Cautions have to be taken to prevent its manipulations and distortions so that it remains wedded to the purpose for which it was initiated. It remains an effective intervention in the protracted struggle of *dalits* against inequality. Special measures of redress are still needed for those having collectively endured social abuse and psychological injury. Structurally organised and traditionally legitimised inequality in order to be eliminated needs its presence in a setting that seems to have failed in pulling the larger society loose from long-established patterns of socialization and social values.

II

Special cushion in the form of protective discrimination subsequently found many new claimants. The accommodative sweep of the policy had to be broadened to accommodate the aspirations of the recently raised in the power structure. Competing interests of the dominant and assertive have found articulation in proliferating claims to the benefits of reservation. Having arrived at the centre in the wake of extending accommodation in democratic processes the intermediate castes claimed a proportionate increase of their share in the power and pie in the Indian society. It indicated a situation where a number of castes inducted only recently from the periphery to the centre of political universe refused to be the appendage of the main contenders in power politics—the upper castes.[13]

The coming together of these castes is not a simple exacerbation of the parochial activities of narrowly circumscribed lesser identities and undissolved residue of traditionalism. It marks a clash between the established and the emerging holders of power.[14] Claims for share in State-controlled jobs that provide limited but crucial outlets for "the progeny of an economically lethargic ruling class" seem to indicate their opposition to its retention among the embedded few. Such sections sought to lift themselves up without taking resort to rank concession syndrome that used to be their earlier strategy for status elevation. The 'Other Backward Classes' are constituted of intermediate peasant castes having low location in the traditional stratification system. Such sections on account of traditions are laggards in pursuit of education and have poor representation in bureaucracy and professions including those of distinctions. Located at a higher rung in the social ladder these castes are endowed with superior resources as compared to the scheduled castes. Social and cultural inhibitions are less serious in their case. Clustering of sources of deprivation are not discriminating to the intermediate castes in the manner they are for the scheduled castes. Constraints are not severe in their case, as they are not afflicted to discrimination involved in exteriority. Placed between the higher castes and the scheduled castes, the affluent among them are ruthless in the exploitation of the wretched on the earth. Professional and bureaucratic elite emerged from among them even in absence of the State policy of protection. Thus the 'new reservation' signifies unrestrained preference for that section of the society that is not distantly worse off. They are less deserving as compared to the bottom groups of the society. Protective discrimination initially had the intent to ensure social and economic equality to favour the weak and the stigmatised. Its shift in favour of intermediate castes had the purpose to incorporate the aspirations of the ascendant intermediate castes. Reservations for the scheduled castes and scheduled tribes were 'directed towards advancing social and economic equality'; reservation for other backward castes is to maintain a balance of power.[15] Status of depressed class seems to have facilitated the economic prowess of the community as lowering of status and class interests favour these bullock capitalists.[16]

The availability of protective discrimination to the other backward castes has been subjected to sharp criticism. It is considered to be the villain of the peace as it exacerbated old divides and fissures. It seems to have fuelled social conflict and unrest on a larger and destructive scale. Such provisions for the intermediate castes it is said lead to restoration and solidification of the caste barriers reversing the process aimed at its erosion. Polarisation of primordial identities is, however, a necessary feature of democracy with developing economy and competing interests. Tensions and violence are necessary accompaniments of stirrings seeking erosion in the embedded equilibrium of dominance.

The new reservation is opposed for its disastrous consequence to pursuit of excellence. Lowered standards in recruitment lead to lowered standard of efficiency and soft corridor of recruitment keeps the society deprived of the services of the most competent persons.[17] Roster of castes in the bureaucracy and profession of distinctions has been criticised as it is opposed to norms of merit and impartiality. Reservation for the 'forward non-twice born communities' is said to have 'laid the foundation of a society in which caste and backwardness replace merit and effort'.[18] Such criticisms, however, tend to ignore the continuous use of merit as an euphemism for self-perpetuating privileges and private aggrandisement. In fact it is difficult to gloss the manipulation of the norm of 'merit' by the privileges to appropriate the retention of resources old and new. In fact the situation of closed privileges in an open system led those with unfulfilled aspirations to stir for reservation. Implementation of policy contents of new reservation however brought into sharp focus the in-built contradictions. Disparities tend to be abrasive. Claims for benefits ensured in protective discrimination have ushered intra-community competitiveness. Contest accompanies policies aimed at sponsoring mobility. Interests of the chosen few seem to find better attention in measures to ensure group mobility. Each caste seeks larger share in areas where it is under-represented without allowing accommodation to those who are compelled to maintain a marginal presence. It is maintained that the real underprivileged do not benefit much as in its implementation it seems to serve the interests of the waferthin affluent upper crust among the middle range castes who tend to perpetuate backwardness to avail benefits in their externally imposed inferiority. Such aspirations oriented to serve the selfish interests in spite of being "a universal phenomenon in all reformist remedies"[19] deserve concern as it "vitiates the quest for fraternity and gives affirmative action rather a bad odour"[20].

Its reliance on caste as the sole criterion for reservation is questioned as it is considered contrary to the fundamental principle of social justice.

In fact to some it amounted to legitimation of caste system through State action. Such tendencies have been considered "repugnant to democracy" and "inimical to the creation of the desired casteless and classless society" and are "contrary to the first principle of social justice in their fairness to the other people".[21] Emergence of a system where merit is at a discount and the link between competence and reward is tenuous does immense harm to crucial institutions. It thus remains parochial in its colour and philosophy. Claiming legitimacy from the national commitment to ameliorate the conditions of the lowest, the unrestrained preference of this not so drastically worse off section of the society seems to have inaugurated a regime of communal allotment. Hierarchical mind perpetuates itself as traditional cleavages are used for secular gains. Politics in a bid to usher parity between castes is likely to turn public institutions into multi-caste panchayats. Opponents of compensatory discrimination consider the extension of the 'pernicious' strategy of support to the other backward classes to be 'a negative turn into backwardness'.[22] Specially its availability to the upper backwards is termed snobbish and unjust seeking transformation of political expediency into a universal truth.[23]

Legitimacy and efficacy of such a programme is highly controverted on account of untampered radicalism and partisanship evident in preparation of recommendations and guidelines on reservation for the other backward castes. This has been criticised for its lack of reliability. Sectarian interests forced it to adopt a methodology for identification of the beneficiaries that is said to be "erratic, whimsical and politically loaded".[24] It ignored the suggestions that the experts associated with it made as it dumped the weightage for various criteria suggested by the experts and came up with its own weightage.[25] It is also maintained that it "made up its mind about its basic recommendations before it started its deliberation".[26] In order to serve the selfish political interest, it is alleged to have 'exaggerated the number of other backward classes and overplayed the backward and underplayed the forward elements in identifying most of the backward castes'.[27] Conclusions arrived with erroneous methodology and unreliable sample designs cannot be basis for scientific observation. Processed data that constituted the foundation to identify backwardness are not available. The commission tended to be selective in accepting precedents thus impairing the sanctity of law. These all in turn reflected "undaunted rush on the part of the capitalist farmers (the core of which is constituted by the intermediate castes in many parts of the country) to seize the administrative power in the political amphitheatre" dominated by the anarcho-syndicalist new-Gandhian ideology.[28] Some of the references quoted in support of the recommendations have been found to be non-existent. Constraints of resources and trained manpower and time led the Mandal Commission to condition itself to practical considerations and realities of field conditions.

III

Comprehensive claims for quota seem to be emerging as competitive interests of the dominant and find articulation in proliferating claims to the benefits of reservations. Compensatory doctrine is inclined to increase its presence and spread. Denial of benefits of protective discrimination to the Christians of scheduled caste origin has provoked resentment to the entire Christian community. The relevance of religion in determining backwardness is questioned. Similarly several constraints and inhibitions led to stagnation of women at the periphery of society. Their representation remains sparse in public life. Patriarchal values are unfavourable to women's initiation into extra-domestic pursuit. Taking this into account the provisions have been made to ensure their representation in the third tier of governance. Similar provisions are demanded for their representation in the other two tiers of governance. Reservation thus seems to be an unavoidable necessity. We however need to have a fresh look at the provisions for protective discrimination to come out of the tangled skein that afflicts it on account of its expanding scope and structure. A social policy to facilitate an intimate rapport between provisions for affirmative protection and extent of deprivation is required. Single list for entitlements of benefits of protection incorporating classification of clientele is desirable. Succour has to be provided in proportion to the degree of deprivation. Loose conceptualization distorts the purpose. The dominants have to be separated from the marginalised to receive priority. Entitlement for statutory protection has to be scientifically decided. Logical and rational procedures are required to be evolved for identification of the beneficiaries. Weighted index of backwardness is to be evolved to determine disadvantages for individual cases. Differential application of the policy seeking to orient it in tune with nature of source deprivation is needed to make State protection context relevant.[29]

Exclusion of those having already benefited is necessary to facilitate inclusion of the lowest and uncared. Entry of 'repeat group' is to be avoided. The beneficiaries of such State-supported mobility programmes "owe it to the society to put their newly acquired social talents back into the collective pool".[30] Exit system to exclude the privileged is however not to be used in such a way as to defeat the intent of the needed structural transformation of society by denying to the deserving their due. Institutional and procedural safeguards have to be strengthened to stem improprieties and distortions. Its unlimited spread has to be discouraged. The tendency to lean on crutches is not desirable. Reservations are to be eliminated, not perpetuated. It has not to be the primary tool to eliminate discrimination as it can only supplement other strategic options to confront a situation of economic marginalisation and social exploitation.

REFERENCES

1. D. L. Sheth, 'Reservation Policy Revised', *Economic and Political Weekly,* Vol. 22, No. 46, 1987.
2. Bhikhu Parekh, 'A Case for Positive Discrimination' in *Democracy Difference and Social Justice,* (ed.) by Gurupreet Mahajan, Oxford University Press, 1998.
3. Marc Galanter, *Competing Equalities,* Oxford University Press, Delhi, 1984.
4. S.R. Maheshwari, *The Mandal Commission and Mandalisation: A Critique,* Concept Publishing Company, New Delhi, 1991.
5. Marc Galanter, *op. cit.*
6. Dushkin, Lelah, 'Scheduled Caste Politics' in *The Untouchables: In Contemporary India,* ed. by Michael Mahar, The University of Arizona Press, Tuscon, Arizona, 1972.
7. Marc Galanter, 'Pursuing Equality' in *Social and Economic Development in India,* ed. by Dilip K. Basu and Richard Sission, Sage Publications, 1986.
8. Ghanshyam Shah, *Social Movements in India,* Sage Publications, New Delhi.
9. Andre Beteille, *The Problem,* Seminar, 1981 (December 1981).
10. Dushkin, Lelah, 'Scheduled Caste Politics' in *The Untouchables: In Contemporary India,* ed. by Michael Mahar, The University of Arizona Press, Tuscon, Arizona, 1972.
11. Minoo Masani, Quoted in Marc Galanter's article entitled "Compensatory Discrimination in Political Representation," *Economic and Political Weekly,* Vol. 14, No. 7-8, Feb, 1979.
12. Glen M. Johnson and Sipra Bose, "Social Mobility among Untouchables", in *Cohesion and Conflict in Modern India* (ed.), Giri Raj Gupta, Vikas Publishing House Pvt. Ltd., New Delhi, 1978
13. A.K. Lal, "Politics of Protection" in *Reservation: Policy, Programmes and Issues,* ed. by Vimal P. Shah and Binod C. Agrawal, Rawat Publications, 1986.

14. Atul Kohli, *Democracy and Discontent,* Cambridge University Press, 1991.
15. Quoted by A. Majit, *Mainstream,* 20.10.90, p.14.
16. Llyod L. Rudolph and Susanne H. Rudolph, *In Pursuit of Lakshmi*, Orient Longman, Hyderabad, 1987.
17. S.R. Maheshwari, *The Mandal Commission and Mandalisation*, Concept Publishing Company, New Delhi, 1991.
18. M.N. Buch, 'Reverse Discrimination Against Upper Castes', *Times of India,* October 8, 1994.
19. Government of India, Report of the Backward Classes Commission, GOI, New Delhi, 1980.
20. Dipanker Gupta, 'Recasting reservations in the language of rights' in *Democracy Difference and Social Justice*, edited by Gurupreet Mahajan Oxford University Press, 1998.
21. Acharya Kalekar, Backward Class Commission I Report, GOI, New Delhi, 1955.
22. V.A. Pai Panandikar, 'Introduction' to *The Politics of Backwardness: Reservation Policy in India,* Konark Publishers Pvt. Ltd., New Delhi, 1997.
23. Ramashray Roy, 'Fiction into Fact', *Indian Express*, 30 August, 1990.
24. S.C. Dube, 'A Retrogate Fetish', *Hindustan Times*, 3 September, 1990.
25. B.K. Roy Burman, *Indian Express,* 31 August, 1990.
26. A.M. Shah, 'Double Talk on Caste', *Hindustan Times*, 7 September 1990.
27. B.K. Roy Burman, *Indian Express*, 31 August, 1990
28. B.K. Roy Burman, 'Criteria for Identification of the Backward Classes' in *Social Structure and Change* (iv) ed. by A.M. Shah *et al.* Sage Publications, New Delhi, 1997.
29. T.K. Oommen, 'Elements of Deprivations—Beyond the Mandal Report', *Times of India*, Oct. 22, 1993.
30. Dipanker Gupta, 'Recasting reservations in the language of rights' in *Democracy Difference and Social Justice* edited by Gurupreet Mahajan, Oxford University Press, 1998.

5

THEORY AND PRACTICE OF BSP'S CONCEPT OF SOCIAL JUSTICE
Implications for Politics

SUDHA PAI

The emergence of the BSP since the mid 1980s in UP has introduced into its conservative society new notions of social justice and transformation which are of significance for politics. It is a party of the *dalits* which espouses a concept of "social justice" exclusively for the "*dalit/bahujans*" which it argues will "right historical wrongs" perpetrated against them by the upper castes. Based upon this notion of justice, the party stands for the establishment of a new social and political order in which *dalit/bahujans*, who constitute the majority, will replace the "*manuvadi*" forces which have for long ruled UP. The new social order it believes can only be achieved by "social engineering" from above, i.e. introducing developmental and welfare programmes for *dalit* upliftment using the power and resources of the State, rather than revolution "from below".

The party's notion of retributive justice, which is meant to right historical wrongs, has already led to social and political conflict in UP, particularly during periods of BSP rule, between the *dalits* and the upper and middle castes who are not prepared to give up the social status and political power which they have long enjoyed, and sections of the rural poor who feel they are being neglected by the government. These developments have important implications for not only the social fabric, but the future shape of the emerging party system and politics in the State.

This chapter analyses the theory and practice of the BSP's concept of social justice and its significance for politics. It examines the ideology of social justice of the party, and based upon it, the Ambedkar Model Village Programme which by concentrating the existing State-owned resources for social welfare and development on villages with a high *dalit* population, provides a good example of retributive "social engineering". Moreover, in spite of not being very successful in its implementation, it has attracted widespread attention, and is an important tool of mobilisation by which the BSP hopes to extend its *dalit* base across the State. In the concluding part the implications of these ideas and their practice for politics in the State are discussed.

I

HINDU SOCIAL ORDER AND RETRIBUTIVE JUSTICE

The BSP describes itself as an "Ambedkarite" party and draws upon the ideas of Ambedkar; however, its ideology is largely based on the ideas and speeches of Kanshi Ram. A fundamental tenet of the ideology of the BSP is that the basic divide in India is not class but caste. For thousands of years Hindu society has been divided into two basic groups: the *sawarnas* or upper castes who on the basis of birth have occupied a privileged socio-economic and political position and enjoyed the fruits of the labour of the workers belonging to the low caste *sudras* and *ati-sudras* who have remained poor, illiterate, and occupied a menial social position. Kanshi Ram has argued that the *dalits* form the original inhabitants (*mool nivasi*) of the land who were conquered by the Aryans. The history of ancient India is hence one of opposition and the final victory of the Aryans over the original people who were reduced to untouchables. Since then caste-based conflict has been an enduring reality.[1]

This social order sanctioned by brahminical Hinduism is hence Aryan in origin, propagates an unequal social order and is anti-humanitarian. Based upon falsehoods and religious myths propagated by the upper castes, it has historically rested upon three pillars. First, every caste group has performed certain specified tasks: the upper castes performed the duties of ruling, while the menial tasks were assigned to the lower castes. This division had the sanction of religion and custom, and thirdly emerging from these two, every *jati* has occupied a designated position in the social hierarchy, the untouchables being the lowest placed below the line of pollution.[2]

Brahminism is described by the BSP as a ruling socio-cultural ideology that has succeeded, by dividing the majority into innumerable caste groups, in entering and dominating all aspects of life including politics today. The Hindu religious books and philosophy have also played an important role in spreading falsehoods. Religion should teach and be based upon equality of all human beings, but Hinduism, Kanshi Ram argues, is not a religion but an ideology upholding an unequal social order. As the upper castes were also the ruling classes they succeeded in according this unequal social system legitimacy as the all-India Hindu civilisational and cultural order accepted by all including the lower orders, while in fact, the BSP points out, every *jati* has had its own "*samaj*" or community, there never was it is argued a "Hindu community", the SCs in particular stood outside it and still do.[3] This aspect particularly appeals to the party's supporters in the context of the BJP's attempts to create a single unified Hindu community, and vote-bank based upon it.

The BSP thus has an ideology similar to that of the anti-Brahmin movements of southern and western India, and claims to draw upon all anti-brahminical ideas/movements since Jyotiba Phule. However a fundamental and significant difference is that the anti-brahminism of the BSP is much more political than cultural and all strategies of mobilisation are based upon this fact. The basic aim is to replace brahminical political rule by Bahujan rule, without which it is held social justice is unattainable. Political equality by attaining political power is for Kanshi Ram primary, it assures freedom from social oppression and improves status. For this it is necessary to capture political power, and he has held that "Political Power is the key by which any lock (obstacle) can be opened".[4]

An important position is hence accorded to the State in the thinking of the BSP leaders. They argue that the Indian State which is under the control of brahminical leaders propagates its ideology through its educational system, socialising the younger generation, and thereby ensuring the continuation of the unequal system. Kanshi Ram argues that all leaders and political parties the country has produced are brahminical or "*Manuvadi*" and this is a major stumbling block to social change. Prior to independence the Congress party had promised a State which would respect all religions and stand equidistant from them, but this promise was not kept. In fact the BSP describes the Congress with its upper caste leadership as the most Manuvadi. In such a situation establishment of a "secular State" is impossible unless a party such as the BSP committed to destruction of the brahminical order comes to power.

Even the Constitution which is based upon the principles of equality is ineffective. All policies of the government based upon such thinking have hence prevented uplift of the *dalits* even after independence.

Although the BSP believes in total transformation i.e. destruction rather than reform of the Hindu social and political order, this revolution is to take place not through social upheaval, but the ballot box. Kanshi Ram visualises two stages by which the position of the *dalits/bahujans* would undergo a transformation. The first is capturing power through mobilisation and electoral victory from the Brahmins who comprise only 10-12% of the population. He has consistently tried to make the *dalits* realise that the first past the post system makes it possible for them to come to power, and thereby seize the system from within. In the later Phase the revolution would penetrate deeper into society transforming it.[5] Thus caste which was used by the upper castes for oppression itself becomes the weapon by which it is to be destroyed using the electoral system.

The use of electoral politics is justified because today brahminism itself is dominating due to use of political power. Of the three pillars the first two have been destroyed. The occupational structure is no longer ascribed by birth, and it has been realised by the *dalits* that the caste system does not enjoy religious sanction. The third pillar of inequality and hierarchical order based upon caste, which still exists, rests upon political power. Hence only through politics social change is possible. Whether we establish capitalism, communism or socialism it would make no difference as long the power of the State is in the hands of the upper castes. Even the Communist parties are brahminical, only the BSP as an Ambedkarite party looks after the interests of the *dalits*. Independence in Kanshi Ram's opinion was gained only by the *sawarnas*, in the colonial period the British rulers treated the *dalits* better.

The establishment of a democratic system based upon adult franchise in the post-independence period has helped the *sawarnas*, and parties formed by them, to continue their hold over the social and political system. They have done so by means of vote-banks, money power and false promises. The BSP on attaining power would establish 'real' and 'substantial' democracy, which for Kanshi Ram is rule of the majority i.e., of the *bahujans*. Such a democracy would establish equality, not through crushing the *sawarnas* but on the strength of *bahujan* unity.[6] The BSP sees no difference between the philosophy of Ambedkar, the emancipation of the untouchables, and the ideals enshrined in the Constitution. It believes that socialism can transform Indian society, but major obstacles exist such as caste, and the plurality of languages, religions, and customs which have divided the working class. The new social order would be based upon brotherhood, equality, and humanitarianism. Hence a basic slogan of the BSP, drawn from Ambedkar, is "Educate, Agitate and Organise".

Based upon the common platform of opposition to brahminism, the BSP leadership in the early 1990s evolved the concept of a "Bahujan Samaj" which would unite all sections of the backwards, *dalits*, scheduled tribes, and religious minorities overcoming their caste/class differences in order to upset the existing unequal social order. "Bahujan" symbolised not only majority as described by Phule, but was also conceived as an ideological-cum-electoral strategy that would create the base for empowerment. However, on this aspect, the party remains divided into two factions: those who want to pursue this strategy, and those who argue that the BSP should remain a party/movement of only the *dalits*. The failure of the SP-BSP government in 1995 showed that not only was such a strategy a failure due to competition between the *dalits* and the backwards, but that their notions of social justice differed. As a result in its post-*bahujan* phase which marks its conversion from a social movement to a party, it seeks alliances with even *manuvadi* parties in order to capture power, but once in power its policies of social justice are meant for the *dalits*.[7] Kanshi Ram believes that the lower backwards are not as politicised as the *dalits*, they lack strong leadership and understanding of the need to unite and fight the *sawarnas*. This is the reason why *bahujan samaj* is at present not attainable.

The BSP has tried to justify its alliances with upper caste parties since the mid 1990s, as not constituting a shift from its path of *dalit* justice and upliftment but as short-term strategic alliances. Its leaders, both Kanshi Ram and Mayawati, have argued in their speeches that capturing political power by any means is both necessary and justified in the case of a *dalit* party in UP as without it social transformation is impossible. The upper castes remain conservative and reactionary and are not prepared to concede an equal position to *dalits* whom they still treat badly. Hence it is only by capturing and using State power that *dalits* can introduce social change "from above". Capture of power, however, is only the first step in a democratic system, there remains a hard battle ahead in transforming society.

The BSP is critical of Gandhi and contrasts his views on social justice with those of Ambedkar. Criticism of the Congress and its leaders who long enjoyed the support of the *dalits* in the country is necessary for it to mobilise and politicise *dalits*. Harijan leaders in the Congress are dubbed "*chamchas*". A major argument which justifies the need for the BSP to capture power is that during long years of Congress rule in spite of considerable developments the benefits have not reached the weaker sections. Regarding reservations, long considered a tool of social change by leaders in India, the BSP feels that it is not the way to eradicate inequality, or a permanent solution. Kanshi Ram points out, "I will never approve of a system in which people are made to walk on crutches. What we need is a socio-economic environment in which we can eat, talk, walk, and compete on an equal footing....... Our aim is to create a Bahujan Samaj".[8] For this while mobilisation is vital the ultimate solution is capture of state power.

The economic content of the ideology of the BSP is weak and lacks clarity. While the need for ending poverty and introducing social change is underlined, and a number of required policies mentioned such as land reform nationalisation of industry, need for better wages, modernisation of industry etc., how this will happen has not been worked out. Poverty is seen as the result of social and political powerlessness and rooted in the brahminical system, and not an economic condition to be dealt with by economic policies. Kanshi Ram holds that the prevailing economic inequalities, such as skewed distribution of land and income, are the result of the unequal caste system. For example, it is oppression by upper caste landlords which is the root cause of the unequal relations on land, and ill-treatment of landless labourers. He does not advocate re-distribution of land as this would introduce social revolution which he is keen to avoid. Rather if political power was in the hands of the oppressed they could demand better wages and working conditions and would no longer be badly treated on grounds of their low social status. Economic power according to him is based upon political power. He argues that the unused lands could be utilised to set up large mechanised collective farms on which the landless could work and prosper.[9]

Thus Kanshi Ram seems to be advocating a form of State Socialism though he still believes in the importance of individual property rights. Redistribution of economic assets and social justice can be brought about only by the State, hence capturing power is given so much importance. However, it is a State in which the *dalit/bahujans* are in power that is capable of doing so, not one controlled by *manuvadi* parties headed by upper caste leaders. Firstly, it prevents the *dalits* from being oppressed and gives them a sense of self-respect. Secondly, by introducing policies favourable to them it carries out "social engineering" from above which was not possible earlier. *Dalit* unity and fighting for self-respect using political power is also important as it would stop the upper castes from ill-treating the lower castes and improve the conditions in villages.

What the BSP wants, therefore, is not reform of the system or more social welfare policies as in the past, but a decisive share in political power. The leadership believes that this alone is the way in which they can bring about *dalit* upliftment. The greatest source of power in India today is politics, hence it is only by capturing political power and attempting "social engineering" from above that social justice can be achieved.

II

RETRIBUTIVE JUSTICE IN PRACTICE: THE AMBEDKAR VILLAGE PROGRAMME

The Ambedkar Village Programme (AVP) is the largest development/ welfare programme adopted by the BSP upon attaining political power. It is a good example of a major welfare programme meant almost exclusively for *dalits*, based upon the notion of social justice and "social engineering" from "above" i.e. with the help of State power.

The AVP was begun by the Mulayam Singh Yadav government in 1991 with the avowed intention of gaining *dalit* support in UP following the decline of the Congress party. Under it in every district at the block level, villages with 50 per cent *dalit* population were selected and special developmental/welfare programmes provided. The AVP was adopted by the SP-BSP government in 1993, and more enthusiastically by the Mayawati governments in 1995 and 1997. The latter government lowered the required *dalit* population to 22 to 30 per cent thereby covering more villages. Under the 73rd Amendment, reservations for weaker sections have also been provided in Panchayat institutions at all levels. If the majority of persons in a village are *dalits* or BCs then the Pradhan of the Gram Panchayat, and the chairperson of the Block Development Samiti must be from one of these communities, preference always being given to the former. The capture of political power by the BSP, reservations for *dalits* in Panchayat bodies and politicisation of *dalits* in UP have together provided a fertile field for the success of this scheme in some parts of the State.

Between 1991 and 1997-98 a total of 25,434 Ambedkar villages all over UP have been selected on the criterion described above. The numbers range from 6 villages in some districts to 260 in district Azamgarh where there is a concentration of *dalit* population. It is important to note that while these villages have been selected, developmental work under the various schemes has not been begun in the case of all.[10]

Under the AVP schemes such as road building, drinking water etc., have been put into operation, or already existing ones such as the IRDP, JRY adopted and more funds provided. Under IRDP, loans are provided for buying buffaloes, for dairying, poultry, beekeeping, mushroom cultivation, setting up shops and other small businesses. As jobs cannot be provided under JRY in the village, the funds granted are used for village improvement, such as building brick roads, drains, schools and Panchayat buildings etc. Two housing programmes — the Indira Awas and Nirbal Awas Yojanas, and old-age pension schemes are also part of the programme. Many of the schemes, such as drinking water pumps and wells, are undertaken in the *dalit* section of the village. The programmes are selected and administered by the Gram and Block panchayats under the new decentralised Panchayat system.[11]

The recent Mayawati government (March to September 1997) has claimed that all the incomplete schemes begun between 1991 and 1996-97 in 11,524 Ambedkar villages, have been successfully completed during its tenure. In these villages, 37 schemes considered important to improve the quality of life of a village have been undertaken. Of these 37, 11 schemes have been identified as central and essential for every Ambedkar village, such as link roads, electrification, drainage, brick roads inside the village, free boring scheme for irrigation, housing, drinking water, and various educational programmes. The government held that between 1991 and 1996-97 in 1,582 villages link roads have been built, 1,166 electrification completed, 73,783 sulabh latrines built, 3,916 drainage work has been completed, and 46,934 houses for *dalits* built etc.[12] A sum of Rs. 358 crores has been spent, and during the year 1997-98 it is proposed to spend Rs. 700 crores on the selected villages.

While it can be argued that the programmes undertaken are not new, many of them such as road building and electrification will improve the lives of all villagers, and *dalit* upliftment schemes have been pursued since independence, some features of the AVP must be noted. Firstly, these programmes are being executed by a government "of the *dalits*" in villages with a sizeable *dalit* population who would directly derive benefit from them; secondly, the budget for these programmes is very large, some of the programmes such as housing and land distribution are only for *dalits*, and even others such as loans under the IRDP have been given largely to the latter. By it the party hopes to improve the lives of 92 lakh SC/ST persons in the State.[13]

Thirdly, the model AVs are being built by transferring funds from developmental schemes spread over larger areas and concentrating them in small enclaves for the *dalits*. On assuming power in 1995, the Mayawati government issued orders to stop all social welfare programmes so that funds could be diverted to the selected Ambedkar villages, and all officials were instructed to give maximum attention and priority to such villages.[14] During the tenure of the BSP both in 1995 and in 1997, many senior officials at the State, district and even block level have been from the *dalit* community, and it was hoped this would help in implementation of such programmes.

After the failure of the SP-BSP coalition, and fall of the Mayawati government formed with BJP support in 1995, until the resumption of power by the BSP in 1997, the AVP was not given importance. On assuming power in March 1997 Mayawati issued orders that all important programmes must immediately be operative in the selected Ambedkar villages. It also issued orders in contravention of existing government policy that from the existing funds all sanctioned schools must be opened in Ambedkar villages, and only after all such villages were covered others were to be considered, and it expected a report on this scheme by 30th September. Even schools already sanctioned in other villages were not to be set up.[15] Thus having achieved power, the BSP tried during its six-month tenure to provide maximum possible benefits to *dalits* under the AVP. In September 1997, it was one of the reasons why after six months in power, the BSP was keen that the BJP government under Kalyan Singh should continue its social policies. Finally, a significant characteristic of this programme is that it has been advertised by the BSP as a unique experiment as it aims at upliftment and social justice for those who have so far been treated unjustly by society.

In some parts of the State the AVP has been successful and introduced a qualitative change in the lives of villagers. Field reports show that this has happened mainly in parts of Western UP, such as Meerut district, where the Chamars/Jatavs are supporters of the BSP and consequently highly politicised, and taking advantage of the reservations to local panchayats, have gained some control over the schemes provided under the AVP.[16]

Reports from other parts of the State show that very little change has taken place. In Rae Bareli district, for example, only a few houses have been built under the Awas Yojana, and neither link roads nor electrification has been provided. The president of the All India SC Employees Welfare Organisation, in a letter to the CM of UP, has alleged that in spite of 198 Ambedkar villages being selected in Rae Bareli district no change has taken place. Complaints to the local officials have had no effect.[17] In Mohanlalganj district Village Kudha, there is still no road making entry into the village difficult during the rains, children have to commute very far to a high school, there are only a few handpumps and poor irrigation facilities, in spite of being designated an Ambedkar village.[18] Apathy and corruption on the part of bureaucrats is the usual reason cited by villagers who are however aware of the programme. In East UP too, the scheme has not so far had an impact. However, if the BSP could come to power for a full term of five years, its ideal of social justice for the *dalits* could perhaps be achieved to a greater extent.

III

IMPLICATIONS FOR POLITICS

The social policies of the BSP, based upon its concept of retributive justice, have contributed to the ongoing conflict among major caste groups in UP. The BSP's concept of social justice and methods to achieve the same appeal to a new post-independence, educated, upwardly mobile, identity conscious, and highly politicised generation which has arisen in parts of UP largely among the Chamars/Jatavs—paradoxically due to State policies since independence. They have also experienced a socio-cultural process of "Ambedkarisation" and voting and supporting the BSP is seen as part of this process. Unlike an older generation who remains subservient to the upper castes and earlier supported the Congress, the younger generation is aggressive and ready to fight for what they perceive as righting of historical wrongs. This has led to conflict between the *dalits* and the upper and middle castes, who do not like the new assertiveness shown by the former since the rise of the BSP, and who are opposed to any social change which would affect their position. The Brahmins and the Rajputs, the two upper castes, who had earlier supported/voted the Congress, have since the late 1980s transferred their allegiance to the BJP, and are unhappy about the coalition formed by the latter with the BSP.

The failure of the SP-BSP coalition, based upon the ideal of creation of *bahujan samaj* in 1993, shows the differing caste/class interests and rivalry in the countryside between the middle caste backwards and the *dalits*. In the first five months of the coalition government there were about 60 clashes between the two groups. Together with the Harijan (Prevention of Atrocities) Act, welfare policies were one of the issues which contributed to differences between the two parties. In October 1995, SP workers protested that the new Mayawati government, formed with the support of the BJP, by diverting funds to Ambedkar villages was creating divisions within villages and opposed it.[19] The new government had issued orders that primacy was to be given to establishment of primary schools in Ambedkar villages over all others leading to diversion of funds, which was in contravention of the orders of the Mulayam Singh Yadav government which had held that a school was to be set up in each village.

On the other hand the policies of social justice of the BSP have created alienation and discontent among the non-*dalit* rural poor, particularly the Most Backward Caste groups such as the Dhivars, Jogis Kumhars, barbers, etc. Perched precariously on the border dividing the clean and the unclean castes in the social hierarchy, they are large in number and found all over the State as they were earlier landless service castes forming part of the *jajmani* system. These groups, who have only recently become politically conscious, feel that only a small section of 'forward groups' among the backwards such as the Yadavs, Kurmis, Gujars etc., benefited under the rule of both the Congress and the BLD/LD while they remained backward. Similarly during the period of BSP rule in spite of the fact that they are one of the poorest groups, a major share of the benefits of the social policies of the government under the AVP such as loans, housing, handpumps, wells, toilets etc., have gone to the *dalits* many of whom particularly the Jatavs, are economically better-off than them. Moreover with the introduction of reservations in panchayat institutions, *dalit* pradhans have preferred to help their own community. The Jatavs, on the other hand, are reluctant to share the benefits of welfare programmes with the MBCs, because the latter in spite of sharing common economic interests still treat the former as "untouchables" standing lower than them in the caste hierarchy.

Even within the *dalit* community there is conflict over equitable distribution of welfare programmes. The AVP has helped the emerging entrepreneurial and upwardly mobile groups such as the Jatavs, rather than the really poor and deserving such as the Balmikis or Pasis. Our field study shows that in Meerut district in fact the Jatavs have used the programme to improve their own position vis-a-vis the middle castes.

These conflicts over social status and scarce resources in the civil society of UP are reflected in the political preferences of various social groups and underlie the inability of any party to gain a majority. The Congress Party occupied a significant position in UP till the mid 1980s and was able to gain the support of the upper and lower castes, and even a section of the middle castes which did not support the backward parties the LD/JD. The decay and internal disintegration of the party in the 1980s, a process which had begun in the late 1960s, provided space for opposition parties such as the BSP and the BJP. This together with caste-based mobilisation has led to fragmentation of the social base of parties along caste lines creating violent confrontation both at the grass-roots and in politics. The upper castes and the *dalits* have found an alternative in the BJP and the BSP respectively, to which they have transferred their allegiance, while the upper backwards support the SP. The MBCs earlier supported the Congress and with its decline due to the lack of a party which would help them, they have in many cases drifted towards the BJP. Considering themselves "clean castes" and alienated by the social policies of the BSP, they do not support it. The process of re-grouping of social and political forces following the disintegration of the base of the Congress party is still going on and the BSP's concept of social justice and policies based upon it have contributed to it.

NOTE

This paper is part of a larger project "Democracy and Social Capital in Segmented Societies" funded by SIDA, Sweden.

REFERENCES

1. R.K. Singh, *Kanshi aur BSP Dalit Andolan ka Vaicharik Adhar Brahmanvad Virodh* (Hindi), Govind Vallabh Pant Institute, Allahabad, Kushwaha Book Distributors, Allahabad, 1996:12.
2. Maharaj Singh Bharati, *Kranti ke Panch Khambe* (Hindi), Publisher Lalji Pal, Kanpur (No date):1.
3. *Ibid.*: 2.
4. C.L. Maurya *et al.*, *BSP Supremo Kanshi Ram Press Ke Samne* (Hindi), Kushwaha Publishers, Allahabad, 1996: Introduction.
5. Kanshi Ram, *The Chamcha Age: An Era of Stooges*, privately printed, New Delhi, 1982.
6. R.K. Singh, No. 1:25.

7. Sudha Pai, "Dalit Assertion in UP: Implications for Politics", *Economic and Political Weekly*, September 13, 1997: 2313-2314.
8. *Surya India,* Vol. 16, No. 2, April 1992 (English edition).
9. R. K. Singh, No. 1:37.
10. Records, Ministry of Welfare, Government of UP, Lucknow, 1997.
11. Sudha Pai, "Panchayati Democracy and Social Capital: A Study of Three Ambedkar Villages in Meerut District". Paper presented at the 2nd Conference of the Project "Democracy and Social Capital in Segmented Societies" at Johannesburg, South Africa, 12-17 October, 1997 (Forthcoming).
12. "Major Policies and Programmes Undertaken by the Mayawati Government" (In Hindi). Pamphlet issued by Department of Information and Public Relations, Government of UP, Lucknow, 20th September, 1997, 10-12.
13. *Ibid.: 12.*
14. *Dainik Jagran* (Hindi), Lucknow, October 4 & 6, 1995.
15. *Dainik Jagran,* Lucknow, September 30, 1997.
16. Sudha Pai & Jagpal Singh, "Politicisation of Dalits and Most Backward Castes: Study of Social Conflict and Political Preferences in Four Villages of Meerut District", *Economic and Political Weekly*, June 7, 1997: 1356-1361.
17. *Dainik Jagran*, Lucknow, September 23, 1997.
18. *Dainik Jagran*, Lucknow, September, 28, 1997.
19. *Dainik Jagran*, Lucknow, October 5, 1995.

6

PROTECTIVE DISCRIMINATION
How Much Relevant, How Much Obsolete?

S. K. PANT

"Nurse the Baby, Protect the Child and Free the Adult."
—Professor D. M. Nanjundappa, 1986

Introduction

Protective discrimination, or the reservation, as the name connotes could be described as the protection given by discrimination. In other words, it aims to provide an element of protection, security to a particular section or a segment of the society who have been found to be socially and economically weak, thereby, incapable of participating and contributing to the development of the region or the State. Thus by extending the cover of protection, the government ensures that their self-interests are safeguarded and they come forward to participate, through various welfare schemes and programmes, into the mainstream of development.

Another important characteristics of protective discrimination is that it is not an area-specific or a region-specific problem. In fact their ramifications are well spread out and are transnational. In that sense, it could be called to be truly universal phenomenon; however, its nature and form may have different meaning and contexts.[1]

It is said that protective discrimination has three major components viz. (i) political participation component, (ii) the educational component and (iii) the economic activity and occupational component as these components are supposed to be the direct approaches that facilitate the participation of individuals or groups into the mainstream of developmental activities.

The Concept

The concept of protective discrimination has not been a new one. In fact, its roots could be traced back to our ancient past when the society was divided on caste lines wherein each caste's duties and functions were predetermined or specific and transgression of duties and functions, by and large, was not accepted and permitted. The whole set-up had societal approval. The ultimate fallout of this practice was that a particular community, which has now been classified in the ninth schedule of our Constitution and is generally referred to as the Scheduled Castes, was deliberately deprived of many of the essential services which, in today's context, are thought to be quite essential for the upliftment of an individual or a society.

Offshoot of the Practices

The years of suppression and harassment have moulded this class of society into such an organic entity, which is bereft of aspiration, ideals, enthusiasm, vision and other social traits. Their economic condition and social hierarchical position has, by and large, remained unaffected and they continue to live in a state of deprivation at the bottom. Even the attempts made by various social reformers in the pre-independence period, from time to time, could not mitigate their lot probably on account of the fact that these efforts were too sporadic and also lacked the requisite amount of thrust that was necessary to tackle the problem of this gigantic nature.

The phenomenal growth achieved through years of planning has not succeeded to ameliorate their hardship, as the fruits of development have not been uniformly distributed. All this has pushed this class virtually onto the brink of disaster and they are feeling increasingly marginalised. Protective discrimination, in that sense, has so far failed to provide social justice to the scheduled castes and other weaker sections of the society[2]

Another disturbing outcome of this policy has been the overall performance of the beneficiaries i.e. those set of households who have benefited from it, their performance was found to be highly disappointing and not up to the mark, thereby causing a great deal of embarrassment and problems to the academicians, planners and the administration.[3]

States' Endeavour

Thus after attaining political independence, efforts to ensure social justice to these deprived sections were kept at the top of the agenda. Accordingly necessary provisions were incorporated in the Constitution to enable and empower the State to promote the educational and economic interests of scheduled castes, scheduled tribes and other weaker sections of the society. It was also stated that the State would ensure that this class was given protection from social injustice and all forms of exploitation. Accordingly a certain proportion of seats was earmarked for them in these crucial areas.

It was also realised that by empowering them with education and also taking care of them economically, their status (socio-economic) would also receive the much needed fillip as these ingredients were assumed to be of vital significance for (total) upliftment of human beings. It is, however, relevant to state that this reservation was initially to be given for ten years only. However, at the end of tenth year when it was observed that scheduled castes and other deprived sections could not show the desired amount of progress, as was envisaged of them this period was given another extension of ten years. Since then the policy of protective discrimination is being continuously extended and the pretext given each time has always been the same. Of late, attempts have also been made to raise the quota of their seats which created a lot of heart-burning among the other castes and they resorted to violent means to vent out their frustration and the situation became highly sensitive and very charged. It, therefore, becomes quite pertinent to examine whether the policy of protective discrimination has affected these deprived sections of the society in general and the scheduled castes in particular, whether the policy needs to be continued in the present form or needs suitable modifications or now the time has finally arrived to bid adieu to it.

The policy of protective discrimination is being implemented in many areas/sectors. However, it will not be feasible to study and examine its impact in all the sectors. The present exercise, therefore, attempts to study how it has benefited the scheduled castes and scheduled tribes in two sectors namely the education and the employment/occupational sectors but before we do it, it would be quite relevant to see what has been their status in the present day social hierarchy.

Current Status

Ever since the inception of planned development, the welfare of scheduled castes and other weaker sections of the society has always been kept at the core of the planning. Programme after programme have been chalked out, special packages and various other incentives were also provided to these classes so that they get adequate opportunity for development. However, the impact of all these incentives has not been quite productive. No doubt there has been an improvement in the socio-economic conditions of the people in this class but the proportion of beneficiaries has been quite small as compared to their overall size.

The greatest shortcoming of this policy has been its failure to ensure fair and equitable distribution of facilities among different sections of the beneficiaries. The benefits meant for the people at large have remained confined to the few at the top and not percolated effectively downwards as was being envisaged.[4] On account of this only those who had a head start have increased their lead. It has also led to differential development among the scheduled castes and tribes.

According to the Eighth Five-Year Plan, a majority of scheduled castes and scheduled tribes, who nearly form one-fourth of the total population, were living below the poverty line. There has been no visible change in their occupational pattern and they still constitute bulk of the agricultural landless workers, construction workers and workers in unorganised sectors. They also suffer from long period of unemployment and under-employment. Poverty, ignorance and lack of option in employment opportunities etc. facilitate the continuance of their age-old exploitation. A large number of scheduled caste and scheduled tribe students discontinue their studies prematurely before completing the level for which they were enrolled. The dropout rate in 1986-87 for class I-V was 50.79 per cent for scheduled castes and 66.12 per cent for scheduled tribes. In class I to VIII, the dropout rates were as high as 69.15 per cent and 89.19 per cent respectively.

High Incidence of Poverty

Likewise a close perusal of their economic conditions also reveals that there has been no conspicuous change in their lot during all these years of planning and initiation of various schemes that had been specially earmarked for them. Various estimates on the incidence of poverty show that though there has been a decline in the overall level of poverty, the incidence of poverty among scheduled castes and scheduled tribes was still regarded to be very high.

The proportion of population living below the poverty line, as per Eighth Five-Year Plan, was 51.2 per cent in 1977-78 which subsequently declined to 40.4 per cent in 1983-84 and finally to 33.4 per cent in 1987-88. This proportion in the case of scheduled castes and scheduled tribes declined from 64.6 per cent and 72.4 per cent to 44.7 per cent and 52.6 per cent respectively, during the same period. In other words, the fruits of development have yet not reached the core of this section (Table 6.1).

Table 6.1: Incidence of Poverty

(Percentage)

Year	*Total Population*	*Scheduled Castes*	*Scheduled Tribes*
1977-78	51.2	64.6	72.4
1983-84	40.4	53.1	58.4
1987-88	33.4	44.7	52.6

Source: Eighth Five-Year Plan.

Further, it could also be stated that though the incidence of poverty among the scheduled castes and other backward or weaker sections of the society has gone down, the proportion of households living below the poverty line, however, was still very high as compared to the proportion of households living below the poverty line belonging to the other groups. Such a situation could only arise if the scheduled castes and other weaker sections have not been able to participate in the programme specially designed for them, or they do not consider these programmes to be theirs as according to them they are unrealistic and not based on the ground realities. All this makes these programmes like rituals which are executed at regular frequencies at the behest of some people at the top who have some vested interest. It is like providing a life-support system to a patient without his consent and forcing him to become more dependent and its subsequent withdrawal hurls them back to their quagmire.

The Educational Scenario

The study of educational aspects of scheduled castes and scheduled tribes does not provide an encouraging trend. There can be little denying that educational facilities in terms of physical infrastructure and teachers appointed have undergone a phenomenal change. Diffusion of schooling to every nook and corner has taken place and literacy level of the population which was barely 28 per cent in the sixties steadily climbed to 33.80 per cent, 41.2 per cent and 52.21 per cent in 1971, 1981 and 1991 respectively. However, the growth of literacy rate among the scheduled castes and scheduled tribes has been relatively very slow and does not commensurate with the incentive being offered to them. It could be seen that there were hardly about 10 per cent of scheduled castes and 8 per cent of scheduled tribes literate in 1961. Their literacy level also went up to over 37 per cent and 29 per cent by 1991. However, what has been really disturbing has been the fact that the gap between them and the rest of the population has been steadily increasing (Table 6.2)

Table 6.2: Literacy Rate of SC, ST and Rest of Population

				Gap between Rest of population and	
Year	*SC*	*ST*	*Rest of Population*	*SC*	*ST*
1961	10.27	8.53	27.86	17.59	19.33
1971	14.67	11.30	33.80	19.13	22.50
1981	21.38	16.35	41.22	19.84	24.87
1991	37.41	29.60	52.21	14.18	22.61

Source: Eighth Five-Year plan, Census of India, 1991 Series 1.

Similarly, the impact of education on females and children particularly the girl child among this class has also been bare minimum. The above scenario clearly points out towards the fact that mere expansion of educational facilities in rural areas was not a sufficient prerequisite for universal access to education. There has been a close correlation between class structure and socio-economic activities of the people in both the urban as well as rural areas (Eighth Plan: *Ibid*). The above discussion clearly shows the performance of scheduled castes and other weaker sections of the society in the education sector in poor shades. It is really disappointing to note that when special assistance which takes account of their fees, books, admissions and in few cases meals and dress materials, the response coming out is not a promising one.

Among the reasons for non-enrolment of children in the schools in rural areas or their early dropout as revealed by various studies have been the economic compulsion of the families and their children's particularly the girl child role in supplementing their family household income, higher degree of migration associated with this class, the inevitable clash of economic activity more precisely the agricultural operations like harvesting, sowing, plucking of fruits from the orchards etc., and in some regions the fear of high and influential classes to name a few.[5] Along with this, it could also be said that even the concept of education has also not taken roots among this class.

Occupational and Employment Scenario

Another way of visualising the impact of development or the development programmes on the individuals or on the groups could be by studying the change in their occupational and employment structure. It goes without saying that the enhanced level of literacy and economic status also stimulates the process of mobility of workers, thereby affecting the employment and occupational scenario.

The study of occupational structure of scheduled castes and other castes in Uttar Pradesh during the last three decades shows that there has been practically no change in the proportion of workers from scheduled castes forming the cultivators category whereas there has been a sizeable change in the proportion of workers from other category in this class. However there has been a drop of about 3.4 per cent in the agricultural labourers category which implies that there has been a decline in the proportion of agricultural labourers belonging to scheduled castes. The perusal of Table 6.3 also shows that the uprooted class of workers have subsequently moved to non-agricultural sector. Among the factors causing this shift in favour of non-agricultural sector, some could be summarised as the process of industrialisation and structural change which too has not favoured this class[6] and, therefore, should be viewed seriously.

Even in the formal sector despite the reservation policy, the picture emerging is not an encouraging one. According to the Eighth Five-Year Plan, there were around 2.58 per cent of scheduled castes employed in class I, 4.06 per cent in class II, 9.59 per cent in class III and 18.37 per cent in class IV in the year 1971 in the government sector, which itself was quite low as compared to their numerical proportion to total population. However, by 1991 the proportion further, dropped to 2.53 per cent for class I, 2.35 per cent for class II, 4.98 per cent for class III and 6.82 per cent for class IV staff.

However the employment position in the public sector undertakings was marginally better as their overall ratio which stood at 0.52 per cent and 1.54 per cent for class I and class II in 1971 improved to 1.29 per cent and 2.31 per cent respectively in 1991 (Table 6.4).

Table 6.3 : Occupational Distribution of Main Workers by Social Groups in U.P.

(*Percentage*)

Category	*1971*	*1981*	*1993*
A. Cultivators			
Scheduled Castes	43.42 (70.57)	47.70 (77.35)	42.64 (75.63)
Others	61.53 (100.0)	61.67 (100.0)	56.38 (100.0)
Total	57.43 (93.34)	58.52 (94.89)	53.77 (95.37)
B. Agricultural Labourers			
Scheduled Castes	42.17 (315.40)	34.98 (358.77)	38.77 (297.32)
Others	13.37 (100.0)	9.75 (100.0)	13.04 (100.0)
Total	19.95 (149.21)	13.82 (141.74)	18.14 (139.11)
C. Non-Agricultural Workers			
Scheduled Castes	14.41 (57.41)	17.32 (61.90)	18.59 (60.79)
Others	25.10 (100.0)	27.98 (100.0)	30.58 (100.0)
Total	22.62 (90.12)	27.66 (98.86)	27.79 (90.88)

Source: Census Reports

Note : Figures in brackets shows the disparity index with others = 100.
Others refer to non-SC and non-ST population.

Table 6.4 : Percentage of SC Representation in Government and Public Sector Undertakings

(*Percentage*)

Category	*Government Sector*		*Public Sector Undertakings*	
	1971	1991	1971	1991
Class I	2.58	2.53	0.52	1.29
Class II	4.06	2.35	1.54	2.31
Class III	9.59	4.98	—	—
Class IV	18.37	6.82	—	—

Source: Eighth Five-Year Plan, GOI, Planning Commission, New Delhi : 419.

Re-Orientation of the Policy: Need of the Hour

The aforesaid scenario clearly points out to the fact that the policy of protective discrimination, as practised in the present form, has not been able to achieve the desired level of impact. Of course, there have been some changes both at the literacy as well as on the employment and occupational front but these changes have not been in proportion to the amount of measures and provisions. Its impact, by far, has remained confined to a small proportion of population and those households who have benefited from these policies have refused to share the benefits with others as a result of which the much awaited trickle down effect, as was envisaged, has not taken place. This is perhaps, the biggest failure of the programme and calls for serious evaluation and perhaps suitable modification. A proper blending of both protection and exposure may perhaps provide the soothing touch to the aggrieved feelings of both the communities. The programme or policy could not be condemned if it fails to deliver the goods because the fault may also lie in its execution, or selection of the beneficiaries or the monitoring to name a few. It may be worthwhile to recall that our Constitution, which has been described as one of the largest and most comprehensive texts and which was hailed as one of the longest documents ever prepared, has so far been amended close to eighty times despite the fact that it has not even completed fifty years of its implementation! Does it mean that the Constitution was ill-conceived? No, the fact is that our perception, our objectives and our thinking has changed and that required subsequent changes in the Constitution.

Change is a must and should be allowed because continuity is identified as one of the major traits of life and it also projects the tendencies of the humans to develop, accept the challenges in life. Stagnation leads to oblivion and ultimately leads to obliteration. Things which do not change or for that fact refuse to change either perish or become irrelevant with the passage of time and lose their significance. In the changing circumstances, the programme needs to be closely monitored, constantly amended and upgraded so as to make it realistic, penetrating and more relevant. It may be fitting, here, to recall that our 'public sector enterprises' which were once described as the temples of modern India by none other than the first Prime Minister Pandit Jawahar Lal Nehru in the fifties have now proved to be the biggest liabilities on our economy, so much so that we are totally disbanding them and preparing to get rid of them lock, stock and barrel solely because there has been a change in our perception and criteria of measurement. No longer the criteria of 'social service' is being accepted as the principal objective as the emphasis has now shifted to making the resource vibrant and economically viable.

It is said in the therapeutics that if a dose of medicine is administered to a patient on a sustained basis and if the patient fails to respond or if the response is not of the expected level, the next course left for the physician is to change the course of medicine because further treatment with old medicine generally tends to immunize the system of the patient and he fails to respond for ever. It is a high time, we must take stock of the situation and apply shock therapy so that the scheduled caste community wakes up to the challenges and contributes to the overall development of society and the nation wholeheartedly.

REFERENCES

1. Nanjundappa, D. M. Inaugural address on *Reservation: Policy, Programmes and Issues,* edited by V.P. Shah and B.C. Agrawal, Rawat Publishers, Jaipur, 1986.
2. Shah, Ghanshyam "Protective Discrimination Equality and Political Will" in *Reservation: Policy, Programmes & Issues,* edited by V. P. Shah and B.C. Agrawal, Rawat Publishers, Jaipur, 1986.
3. Chitnis, Suma (1986), "Measuring Upto Reserved Admission" in *Reservation: Policy, Programmes and Issues,* edited by V.P. Shah and B.C. Agrawal, Rawat Publishers, Jaipur, 1986.
4. Lal, A. K. "Education among the Scheduled Castes and Scheduled Tribes in Bihar (Mimeogaph), A.N.S. Institute of Social Studies, Patna, 1986.
5. Pandey, Janak; Pant, S.K. and Bhatt, K. N., "Social Assessment Study of District Primary Education Programme (DPEP) in Bhojpur, Rohtas and Muzaffarpur District", G.B. Pant Social Science Institute, Allahabad, 1997: Showeb, M., Education Mobility among Harijans, O.P. Vohra, Allahabad, 1986.
6. Singh, A.K., "Social Structure and Development Process: A Study of Scheduled Castes of Uttar Pradesh (1971-91)," *Man and Development,* Vol. 4, Chandigarh, December 1997.

7

PROTECTIVE DISCRIMINATION AND SOCIO-ECONOMIC PROFILE OF SCHEDULED CASTE POPULATION IN INDIA

RAJ MANI TRIPATHI

Protective discrimination as a strategy for social change is a specific expression of the liberal ideology. This ideology advocates social change in a piecemeal fashion within the existing framework of social institution and prescribes non-violent constitutional, legal and administrative solutions. The Constitution of India, which is premised upon this ideology, sets the society theoretically open and assures equality of opportunity in all realms. "The claim of the individual to welfare is sacred and irrefutable" in such a Constitution, and it "partakes of the character of a natural right".

This has special significance to the scheduled castes, which have been traditionally oppressed and are consequently, underprivileged. They are in theory liberated by the Constitution, and they can now climb up the social ladder and stake their claim to higher status and the accompanying privileges. In view of the prevalence of market conditions, and their past background and present predicaments, the individuals, belonging to this section of society will not be able to compete with those of the other sections. To overcome the impediments in their upward social mobility, they need some prop. The State assumes the role of a generous donor and bears the responsibility for providing the necessary help to uplift them in the form of protective discrimination.

Of course, it is conceded that not all the members belonging to these castes can be emancipated through such State generosity in the realisation of individual right. Hence, the policy of protective discrimination necessarily concentrates on a few members of these castes. Also, since the process of such sponsored, non-violent and piecemeal change is by nature gradual, the emancipation of these castes is necessarily a long-drawn process spread over several generations and decades.

In the present chapter, the author has attempted to identify the existing pattern of distribution and relative strength of scheduled caste population along with demographic, social and economic characteristics.

Scheduled Caste Population

India is still basically rural but has a high and rising population. This is evident by the high total population with 838.58 million people comprising 435.21 million males and 403.36 million females and a density of 274 per square kilometre (1991). In India 138,223 thousand (16.48 per cent) population belongs to scheduled castes. In the following pages, the socio-economic profile of scheduled castes in India is presented.

According to 1991 census the proportion of scheduled caste population to total in India was 16.48 per cent. But there is considerable variation in their proportions from one State to the other. The proportion of scheduled castes varies from the maximum 28.31 per cent in Punjab followed by Himachal Pradesh (25.34), West Bengal (23.62), Uttar Pradesh (21.05), Haryana (19.75), Tamil Nadu (19.18), Union Territory of Delhi (19.05), Rajasthan (17.29), Union Territory of Chandigarh (16.51), Karnataka (16.38), Tripura (16.36), Orissa (16.20), Andhra Pradesh (15.93), Madhya Pradesh (14.55), Bihar (14.5), Maharashtra (11.09), Kerala (9.92), Gujarat (7.41) and the lowest in Assam (7.40) per cent.

In terms of absolute numbers, Uttar Pradesh has 29.3 million scheduled caste population, followed by West Bengal (16.1 million), Bihar (12.6 million), Tamil Nadu (10.7 million), Andhra Pradesh (10.6 million), Madhya Pradesh (9.6 million), Maharashtra (8.8 million), Rajasthan (7.6 million), Karnataka (7.4 million), Punjab (5.7 million), Orissa (5.1 million), Haryana (3.3 million), Gujarat (3.1 million), Kerala (2.9 million) and Assam (1.7 million). Uttar Pradesh and West Bengal together have one-third of the scheduled caste population in India.

Rural-Urban Structure of Scheduled Caste Population

As we have stated that majority of scheduled caste population lives in rural areas and 81.28 per cent population in India is constituted by scheduled castes. There is much variation from State to State in their distribution. The proportion of scheduled castes in rural areas is recorded highest by Himachal Pradesh (93.67 per cent); other States having very high SC population in their rural areas are Bihar (90.98%), Orissa (89.26%), Sikkim (88.58%), Uttar Pradesh (88.21%), Assam (86.18%), West Bengal (84.29%), Tripura (84.16%), Andhra Pradesh (82.69%), Haryana (82.29%), Union Territories of Dadra and Nagar Haveli (82.16%), Punjab (79.45%), Tamil Nadu (78.68%), Madhya Pradesh (78.14%), Karnataka (76.60%), Arunachal Pradesh (70.53%), Maharashtra (63.39%), Gujarat (62.06%), Union Territories of Daman & Diu (61.55%), Pondicherry (59.21%), Meghalaya (54.81%), Goa (52.32%), and Manipur (47.72%). On the contrary the lowest percentage of scheduled caste population in rural areas is found in Union Territories of Chandigarh (13.34%) and Delhi (11.57%).

In urban areas scheduled castes are less numerous as there is only 18.72 per cent of total urban population of the country constituted by scheduled caste population. The highest per cent proportion of SC population was recorded in Union Territories of Delhi and Chandigarh (88.43%) and (86.66%) followed by Manipur (52.25%), Goa (47.68%), Meghalaya (45.19%), Pondicherry (40.79%), Daman & Diu (38.45%), Gujarat (37.94%), Maharashtra (36.61%), Mizoram (34.01%), Arunachal Pradesh (29.47%), Karnataka (23.40%), Madhya Pradesh (21.86%), Tamil Nadu (21.32%), and Punjab (20.55%). On the contrary, in Himachal Pradesh State only 6.33 per cent of its total urban population is SC population. There are 12 States in the country where percentage of scheduled castes is below 20. Among them Rajasthan (19.79%), Kerala (18.52%), Dadra & Nagar Haveli (17.84%), Haryana (17.71%), Andhra Pradesh (17.31%), Tripura (15.84%), West Bengal (15.39%), Assam (13.82%), Uttar Pradesh (11.79%), Sikkim (11.42%), Orissa (10.74%), and Bihar (9.02%).

Growth of Scheduled Caste Population

The scheduled caste population of India was 51.7 million at the time of independence, which was divided into several groups. It doubled to 104.7 millions—within a period of 34 years by 1981. According to the 1991 census, the scheduled caste population is more than 138.2 millions. With the growth of industrialisation and modernisation there is marked increase in urban scheduled caste population. Nearly 18.72 per cent of the Indian SC population lives in urban areas. Manipur has the highest urban SC population—52.28 per cent. During the 1981-91 period the SC population grew from 104.7 million in 1981 to 138.2 million in 1991. The decadal growth rate of the scheduled caste population has been more than that of the general population during the last decade. The scheduled caste decadal growth rate being 30.99 per cent and that of the general population is 23.79 per cent.

Spatial Distribution of Scheduled Castes

A clear picture emerges when not the total but percentage of scheduled caste population to the total population of the State is considered. Fig. 7.1 and Table 7.1, which depict the percentage of the scheduled caste population to the total population of each State, reveals clearly the pattern of scheduled caste concentration in the country. In such a way all the States and union territories may be classified into five broad categories on the basis of SC population percentage (1991).

Area of Very High Concentration Regions (over 20% SC Population)

The States with very high concentration of scheduled caste population form two distinct regions. First region lies in the North-West and comprises the contiguous States of Punjab (28.31%), Himachal Pradesh (25.34%), Uttar Pradesh (21.05%), West Bengal (23.62%), forms the second region in the Eastern Ganga Plain.

Area of High Concentration Region (15% to 20% of SC Population)

There are three sub-regions of high concentration of scheduled caste population. These are:

(i) *West-Central Zone*: Comprising the State of Haryana (19.75%), Union Territory of Delhi (19.05%) and Chandigarh (16.51%), Rajasthan State (17.29%).
(ii) *South Peninsular sub-region*: Comprising the contiguous States of Karnataka (16.38%), Andhra Pradesh (15.93%), Tamil Nadu (19.18%), and Union Territory of Pondicherry (16.25%).
(iii) *Eastern Isolated Pocket*: Formed by the State of Tripura (16.36%).

Table 7.1: Percentage of Scheduled Caste Population in India (1991)

	State/Union Territory	*Total SC Population*	*Percentage Total*	*Rural*	*Urban*
1.	Andhra Pradesh	10592006	15.93	82.69	17.31
2.	Arunachal Pradesh	4052	0.47	70.53	29.47
3.	Assam	1659412	7.40	86.18	13.82
4.	Bihar	12571700	14.5	90.98	9.02
5.	Goa	24364	2.08	52.32	47.68
6.	Gujarat	3060358	7.41	62.06	37.94
7.	Haryana	3250933	19.75	82.29	17.71
8.	Himachal Pradesh	1310296	25.34	93.67	6.33
9.	Karnataka	7369279	16.38	76.60	23.40
10.	Kerala	2886522	9.92	81.48	18.52
11.	Madhya Pradesh	9626679	14.55	78.14	21.86
12.	Maharashtra	8757842	11.09	63.39	36.61
13.	Manipur	37105	2.02	47.72	52.28
14.	Meghalaya	9072	0.51	54.81	45.19
15.	Mizoram	691	0.10	65.99	34.01
16.	Nagaland	—	—	—	—
17.	Orissa	5129314	16.20	89.26	10.74
18.	Punjab	5742528	28.31	79.45	20.55
19.	Rajasthan	7607820	17.29	80.21	19.79
20.	Sikkim	24084	5.93	88.58	11.42
21.	Tamil Nadu	10712266	19.18	78.68	21.32
22.	Tripura	451116	16.36	84.16	15.84
23.	Uttar Pradesh	29276455	21.05	88.21	11.79
24.	West Bengal	16080611	23.62	84.61	15.39
1.	Andaman & Nicobar Islands	—	—	—	—
2.	Chandigarh	105977	16.51	13.34	86.66
3.	Dadra & Nagar Haveli	2730	1.97	82.16	17.84
4.	Daman & Diu	3891	3.83	61.55	38.45
5.	Delhi	1794836	19.05	11.57	88.43
6.	Lakshadweep	—	—	—	—
7.	Pondicherry	131278	16.25	59.21	40.79
	India (excluding J&K)	**138223277**	**16.48**	**81.28**	**18.72**

Source: Census of India 1991, Series I, Union Primary Census Abstract for Scheduled Castes and Scheduled Tribes.

Area of Medium Concentration Region (10 to 15% of SC Population)

This region has medium concentration of SC population comprising the three adjoining States of Bihar (14.5%), Madhya Pradesh (14.55%) and Maharashtra (11.09%).

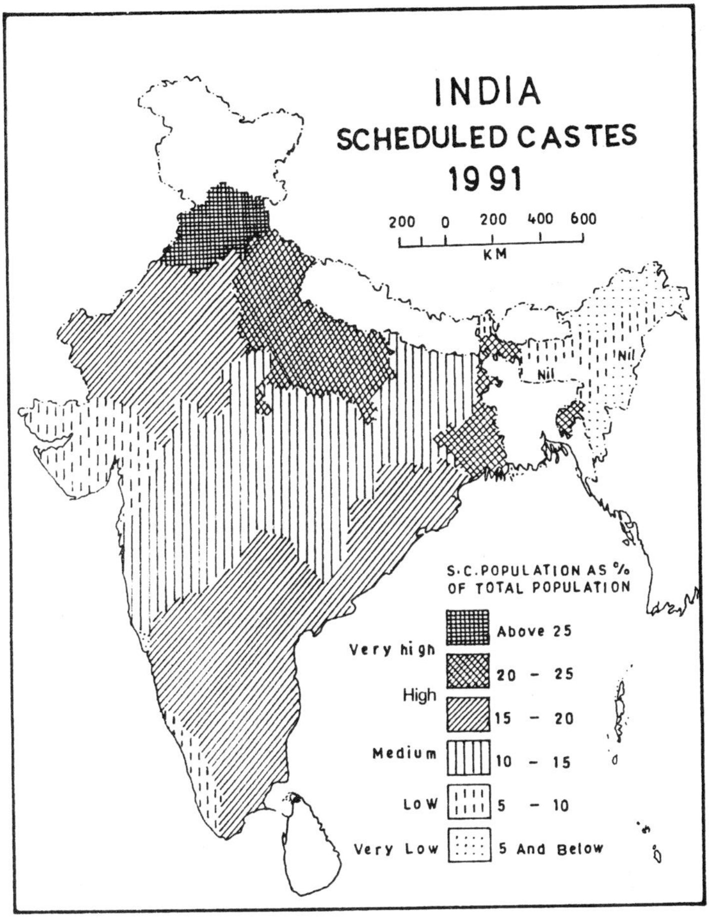

(*Not to the Scale*)

FIG. 7.1

Area of Low Concentration Region (5 to 10% of SC Population)

There are four sub-regions of low SC population lying in three far-flung areas of the country. They are:

(i) Kerala State in the extreme North-East of the country (9.92%);
(ii) A rather extensive region in Western Peninsula comprising the adjacent State of Gujarat (7.41%);

(iii) Assam State (7.40%) in North-Eastern India; and
(iv) The smallest State of Sikkim (5.93%).

Area of Very Low Concentration Region (below5% of SC Population)

Areas of negligible scheduled caste population concentration are confined to two parts of the country:

(i) Firstly, there are the isolated pockets of Goa (2.08%), Daman & Diu (3.83%) and Dadra & Nagar Haveli (1.97%) along the West Coast of peninsular India.
(ii) Second is the North-Eastern region comprising the States of Manipur (2.02%), Arunachal Pradesh (0.47%), Meghalaya (0.51%) and Mizoram (0.10%).

From the foregoing it becomes clear that North-Eastern India with exception of Assam and Tripura is a region with just a trickle of the scheduled caste population.

Sex Ratio of Scheduled Caste Population (Children in age-group 0-6)

The children in the age-group of 0-6 constituted 19.63 per cent of the SC population as against 17.94 per cent for the general population. The scheduled caste population had more children than the general population, which appears to show a higher birth rate among the SC population. The sex ratio for the scheduled caste population was not much different from that of the total population. The respective figures being 922 and 927. The pattern of sex ratio of the scheduled caste population among various States is almost similar to that of the general population of the various States (Fig. 7.2)

Literacy among the Scheduled Castes

As such, when we look at the literacy rates among the scheduled castes of India, we see a rather dismal picture, though there are some bright patches here and there. According to 1991 census the literacy rate of scheduled caste population aged 7 years and above is 37.41 per cent, for male 49.91 per cent and female 23.76 per cent. These figures are much lower than the corresponding figures for the general population. However, the literacy rate of the scheduled caste population has increased from

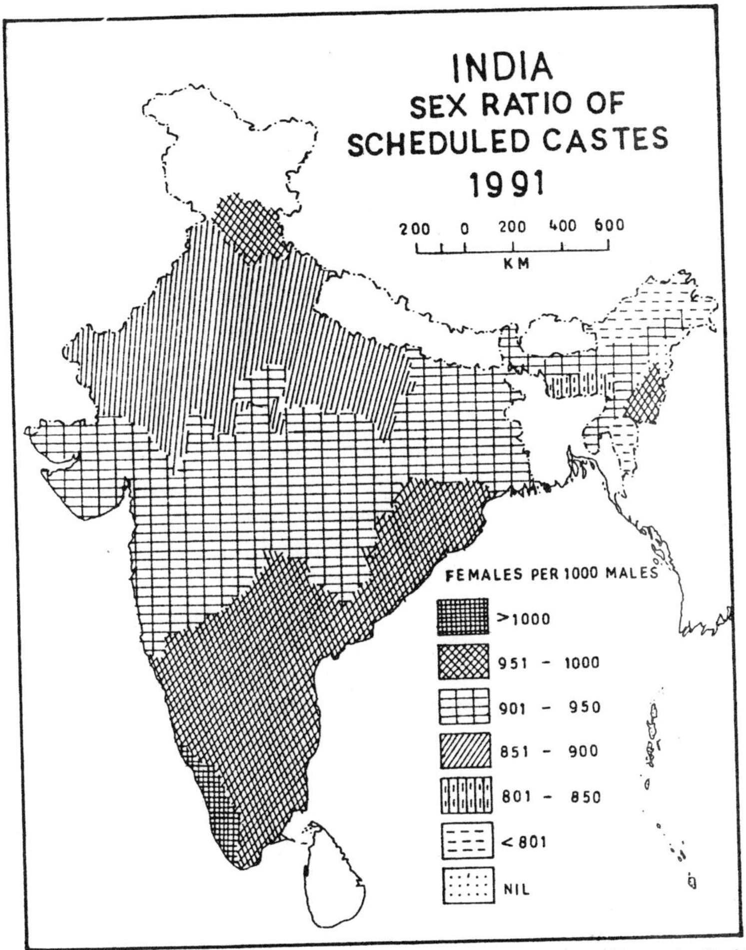

(*Not to the Scale*)

FIG. 7.2

25.82 per cent in 1981 to 37.21 per cent in 1991. In case of males the increase is from 37.67 per cent to 49.91 per cent. While in case of females increase was from 13.0 per cent to 23.52 per cent. The rate of increase of female literacy among the scheduled castes has been much higher over the last decade than the male literacy rate. This is in tune with the trends noticed for the general population. It is, however, seen that the literacy rates for the States of Uttar Pradesh, Bihar and Rajasthan are much lower for the scheduled caste population than that for the general population. The literacy rates for the scheduled caste population and the total population for three States were 26.85 and 41.06 per cent in Uttar Pradesh, 19.49 and 38.48 per cent in Bihar and 26.29 and 38.55 per cent in Rajasthan.

The proportion of literacy among the scheduled caste women was much worse in these States (Table 7.2). The female literacy rates among the scheduled caste population and total population were 10.69 and 25.31 per cent in Uttar Pradesh, 8.31 and 20.44 per cent in Rajasthan and 7.07 and 22.89 per cent in Bihar respectively.

Workers

Occupational structure presents the magnitude of people who are engaged in various economic activities to earn their livelihood. The persons who are not engaged in an economic activity are treated as non-workers or dependants. For the purpose of census of India 1991, all the persons are classified into three broad categories: (i) Main workers, (ii) Marginal workers, and (iii) Non-workers. The main workers are further classified in three broad sectors: Primary, Secondary and Tertiary.

The total number of scheduled caste population was 1382.2 lakh comprising 719.2 lakh males and 662.9 lakh females in 1991. There were 498.7 lakh persons—365.8 lakh males and 132.8 lakh females engaged in economic activities as main workers. Besides this, about 43.7 lakh persons comprising 4.4 lakh males and 39.3 lakh females were marginal workers. Thus the total working force of scheduled castes (main workers + marginal workers) is constituted by 542.5 persons—370.3 lakh males and 172.2 females. However, 39.25 per cent of SC population is workers while this proportion among males and females is 51.48 per cent and 25.98 per cent respectively. (Fig. 7.3)

It is quite evident from Table 7.3 that the work participation rate of the SC population is 39. 25 per cent which is higher than the work population rate of general population (37.46%). This is mainly due to a higher participation rate among the SC women. The work participation rate for SC women being 25.98 per cent as against 22.25 per cent for the general population. In case of males the (WPR) for the SC is 51.48 per cent as against 51.55 per cent for the general population. The female work participation rate among the SC population is much higher than the all-India average in Andhra Pradesh (46.7%), Tamil Nadu (40.9%), Karnataka (36.6%), Maharashtra (36.2%), Himachal Pradesh (35.6%), and Madhya

Table 7.2: Percentage of Literates among Scheduled Caste Population in India (1991)

	State/Union Territory	*Percentage of Total Population*	*Percentage of SC Population*		
			Persons	*Males*	*Females*
1.	Andhra Pradesh	44.09	31.59	41.88	20.92
2.	Arunachal Pradesh	41.59	57.27	66.25	41.42
3.	Assam	52.87	53.94	63.88	42.99
4.	Bihar	38.48	19.49	30.64	7.07
5.	Goa	75.51	58.73	69.55	47.51
6.	Gujarat	61.29	61.07	75.47	45.54
7.	Haryana	55.85	39.22	52.06	24.15
8.	Himachal Pradesh	63.86	53.20	64.98	41.02
9.	Karnataka	56.04	38.06	49.69	25.95
10.	Kerala	89.81	79.66	85.22	74.31
11.	Madhya Pradesh	44.20	35.08	50.51	18.11
12.	Maharashtra	64.87	56.46	70.45	41.59
13.	Manipur	59.89	56.44	65.28	47.41
14.	Meghalaya	49.10	44.27	54.56	31.19
15.	Mizoram	82.27	77.92	77.54	81.25
16.	Nagaland	61.65	—	—	—
17.	Orissa	49.09	36.78	52.42	20.74
18.	Punjab	58.51	41.09	49.82	31.03
19.	Rajasthan	38.55	26.29	42.38	8.31
20.	Sikkim	56.94	51.03	58.69	42.77
21.	Tamil Nadu	62.66	46.74	58.36	34.89
22.	Tripura	60.44	56.66	67.25	45.45
23.	Uttar Pradesh	41.60	26.85	40.80	10.69
24.	West Bengal	57.70	42.21	54.55	28.87
1.	Andaman & Nicobar Islands	73.02	—	—	—
2.	Chandigarh	77.81	55.44	64.74	43.54
3.	Dadra & Nagar Haveli	40.71	77.64	88.03	66.61
4.	Daman & Diu	71.20	79.18	91.85	67.62
5.	Delhi	75.29	57.60	68.77	43.82
6.	Lakshadweep	81.78			
7.	Pondicherry	74.74	56.26	66.10	46.28
	India (excluding J&K)	**52.21**	**37.41**	**49.91**	**23.76**

Source: Census of India 1991, Series 1, Union Primary Census Abstract of Scheduled Castes and Scheduled Tribes.

Pradesh (35.3%). As in case of general population the lowest female work participation rate among the SC has been observed in Punjab (5.4%). It is commonly believed that the female work participation rate is much lower in case of Punjab and Haryana due to the cultural factors and the reluctance among the higher-caste women to report themselves as workers even

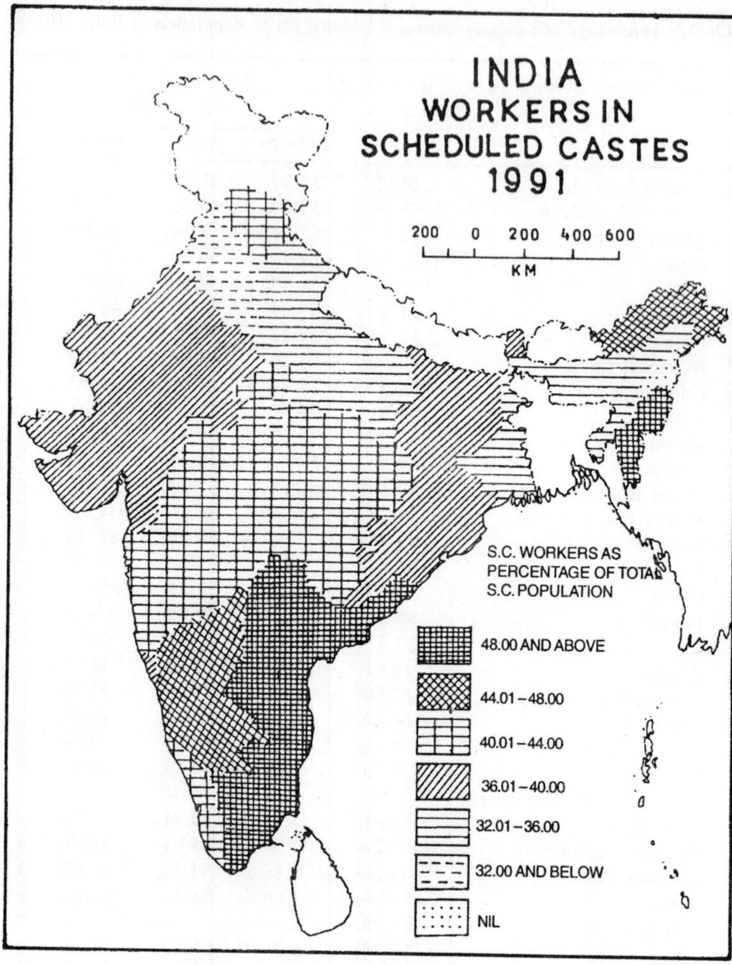

(*Not to the Scale*)

FIG. 7.3

though they may be participant in some economic activity, particularly in the agricultural sector. The low female participation rate among the SC however appears to be surprising in the light of this widely held belief.

The primary activity group is dominated by two other activity groups. The primary activity group constitute 77.11 per cent of SC main workers, 9.83 per cent in the secondary sector and 13.06 per cent in the tertiary sector (Table 7.3). The percentage of main workers in the primary sector

Table 7.3: Percentage of Scheduled Caste Population as Main Workers in India (1991)

	State/ Union Territory	*Total Workers*	*Total SC Workers*	*SC Male Workers*	*SC Female Workers*	*Primary*	*Secon-dary*	*Tertiary*
1.	Andhra Pradesh	45.05	51.08	55.31	46.71	86.52	4.86	8.62
2.	Arunachal Pradesh	46.24	44.27	64.27	12.36	21.70	21.20	57.10
3.	Assam	36.09	34.40	49.36	18.13	66.22	10.09	23.69
4.	Bihar	32.16	37.40	50.11	23.50	89.79	3.52	16.69
5.	Goa	35.28	38.07	49.62	26.12	22.37	36.40	41.23
6.	Gujarat	40.23	37.61	48.39	25.95	55.87	20.18	23.95
7.	Haryana	31.00	30.97	47.59	11.65	64.80	13.68	21.52
8.	Himachal Pradesh	42.83	43.44	51.00	35.63	75.28	12.16	12.56
9.	Karnataka	41.99	44.66	52.40	36.62	78.83	10.43	10.74
10.	Kerala	31.43	41.21	50.96	31.73	69.63	13.12	17.25
11.	Madhya Pradesh	42.82	43.42	50.88	35.27	76.56	12.22	11.22
12.	Maharashtra	42.97	42.82	49.11	36.16	64.07	16.12	19.76
13.	Manipur	42.18	48.96	46.71	30.99	76.94	6.85	16.21
14.	Meghalaya	42.67	35.71	53.64	13.88	29.07	11.54	59.39
15.	Mizoram	48.91	79.16	89.95	10.64	8.00	10.22	81.78
16.	Nagaland	42.68	—	—	—	—	—	—
17.	Orissa	37.53	39.26	54.69	23.44	78.89	7.98	13.13
18.	Punjab	30.88	30.71	52.81	5.40	65.46	12.92	21.62
19.	Rajasthan	38.87	39.26	48.58	28.89	73.96	12.59	13.45
20.	Sikkim	41.51	38.55	49.57	26.80	64.24	21.34	14.42
21.	Tamil Nadu	43.31	48.43	55.78	40.93	81.59	7.66	10.75
22.	Tripura	31.14	28.69	47.43	8.93	63.04	8.30	28.66
23.	Uttar Pradesh	32.20	35.29	50.80	17.61	82.26	7.55	10.19
24.	West Bengal	32.19	33.31	52.03	13.22	72.39	12.00	15.61
1.	And & Nic Islands	35.24	—	—	—	—	—	—
2.	Chandigarh	34.94	32.33	80.80	9.51	3.80	30.68	65.52
3.	Dad & Nag Haveli	53.25	38.94	50.07	26.91	48.58	19.65	31.77
4.	Daman & Diu	37.63	29.43	41.71	17.92	11.10	29.42	59.48
5.	Delhi	31.64	29.25	47.40	7.49	3.06	36.99	59.95
6.	Lakshadweep	26.43	—	—	—	—	—	—
7.	Pondicherry	33.08	40.85	50.99	30.53	72.37	7.97	19.66
	INDIA	**37.46**	**39.25**	**51.48**	**25.98**	**77.11**	**9.83**	**13.06**

Excluding Figures of J&K
Source: Census of India 1991.

among the SC is much higher than that for the general population (67.37 per cent). However, over the last decade there has been a marginal decline in the percentage of main workers in the primary sector by roughly 2 per cent. There has also been a marginal decline in the proportion of main workers in the secondary sector. On the other hand the percentage of main workers engaged in the tertiary sector has increased from 10.78

per cent to 13.06 per cent. This is in consonance with the trend observed among the general population. However it may be mentioned here that roughly half the number (49.06 per cent) of main workers among the SC work as agricultural labourers, whereas in the total population, the agricultural labourers constituted 26.09 per cent only.

Fifty Years of Progress and Current Scenario

A very large number of scheduled castes continue to be socially and educationally backward (literacy rate being 37.41 per cent) as compared to 52 per cent for general population and are languishing at the bottom of the social and economic pyramid, observes the Eighth Plan. During 1977-78 the scheduled caste population below the poverty line was 44.6 per cent which has gone down to 29.9 per cent in 1987-88 as compared to an all-India average of 29.5 per cent. Although there has been an appreciable change in the percentage of population below the poverty line, the incidence is very high. Majority of the scheduled caste population does not hold productive assets or land and constitutes bulk of agricultural workers and works in the unorganised or informal sector. They do not come under the purview of the protective laws like Minimum Wages Act and Prevention of Land Alienation Act. The plan further observes that exploitation of scheduled castes in rural areas whether 'latent' or 'manifest' still continues. Poverty, ignorance, lack of options in employment opportunities and non-existence of organisation which can fight for their right, facilitate the continuance of age-old exploitation. The scheduled caste families have not been able to derive full benefits of development programmes. Among many problems, identification of beneficiaries, poor selection of projects, unrealistic assumption in regard to their viability, administrative cost and leakage are the problems which have been further compounded by largely unresponsive administrative structure.

Although untouchability gets abolished by virtue of Article 17 of the Constitution and its practice in any form is punishable, social discrimination against the scheduled castes in many parts of the country still continues. It is a matter of great concern that in spite of various legal and administrative measures the scheduled caste population still do not feel protected socially and virtually, even after 50 years of independence.

It is needless to say that the cardinal plank of political philosophy of Gandhiji, the Father of the Nation, was to secure social equality for all castes. He worked out a programmatic philosophy not only for achieving political freedom but also for the social and economic backwardness of the masses, particularly the depressed, the poor and the downtrodden. Pandit Jawaharlal Nehru, the first Prime Minister of the country, developed the concept of socialistic pattern of society so that the benefits of economic development reach more and more to the relatively less privileged sections of society, i.e. the scheduled castes and backward classes.

The most significant of the efforts in the new period were the officially sponsored measures of protective-discrimination in different fields: legal (constitutional provisions, enactments etc.); political (reservation in legislatures and lower organs of power etc.); occupational (chiefly job reservations in services); and educational (the various benefit programmes including reservation of seats). This was indeed a tremendous task.

The educational incentives and job reservation of the post-independence period led to considerable social and economic advance among the scheduled castes. Helped by various measures a new elite has emerged among the scheduled castes in different fields and has expanded at its own pace. An important issue in relation to the scheduled castes is their position in society as a result of the gains in the field of education, employment, legal provisions, political pressures etc. operating over the last forty years.

Despite various constitutional directives and a number of legislative and executive measures taken by the Government no clear strategy had emerged for the economic development of scheduled castes prior to the Sixth Plan. A new strategy was evolved during the Sixth Plan which includes three instruments:

(i) special component plan,
(ii) special central assistance, and
(iii) setting up of scheduled caste development corporations.

(1) About 18 States and 3 union territories with sizeable scheduled caste population and central ministers had already formulated their special component plans. A provision of Rs. 8204 crores has been made under the Eighth Plan against Rs. 6205 crores in the Seventh Plan for expenditure under special component plan.

(2) The special central assistance given to the States and union territories for scheduled caste people is linked to Government of India's strategy for the socio-economic development of these

people. This centrally sponsored scheme is the most important programme of the Ministry of Welfare for the alleviation of poverty among the scheduled caste people. The underlying objective behind special central assistance, which provides cent per cent grant to States and union territories as an additive to their special component plans, is that it would be used to give an added thrust to the development programmes for scheduled caste people with reference to their occupational pattern and the need for increasing the productivity of and income from their limited assets by taking up family oriented schemes for them. The SCA is used to fill the critical gaps and vital missing inputs in the family oriented income generating schemes and through non-recurring items so as to make the schemes more meaningful and effective. This theme was started in 1979-80 with a token provision of Rs. 5.0 crores. The State government and union territory administrations are required to disburse special central assistance to various sectors agencies including SCDCs which are involved in the implementation of economic development programmes for scheduled castes. During 1995-96, Rs. 275 crores were released.

(3) The scheduled caste development corporations have been established in the States and union territories with the basic aim of lifting the scheduled caste persons above the poverty line and implement welfare programmes. At present, these corporations are functioning in 19 States and 4 union territories. The central government participates in the share capital investment of the corporations to an extent of 49 per cent. During 1995-96, an amount of Rs. 31 crores was released to the corporations benefiting 5.14 lakh scheduled caste persons.

One may find that there has been a steady improvement in the employment levels of people belonging to scheduled castes in respect to all the four classes of Government services as a result of various measures taken up by the Government of India for the upliftment and welfare of backward and weaker sections of the society. Table 7.4 indicates the present position of the recruitment of scheduled castes in the central services.

Table 7.4: Number of SC Persons (thousand) in Central Government Services

(as on January 1, 1994)

Groups	*1981*	*1983*	*1994*
A - Class I	2883	3574	6046
B - Class II	5298	6368	12443
C - Class III	243028	311070	374758
D - Class IV (excluding Sweepers)	238989	255053	209423
Sweepers	—	—	110569
Total (excluding Sweepers)	490198	576065	602670

Source: India 1975, 1983 and 1996.

Since 1981, the trend has been that all the vacancies reserved for scheduled castes and scheduled tribes are now filled up by the candidates belonging to these communities and there has been no shortfall in annual recruitment to these services.

Conclusion

After 50 years of independence the socio-economic status of SC in the country has no doubt, undergone major change in the recent decades, yet the blind faith and the traditional approaches prevail and dominate the village scene. Through literacy, mutual coordination and inter-family and caste contacts such narrow segregation may be gradually reduced. There should be change of outlook towards labour and vocations and the acquired status must be given due cognition along with the ascribed status already prevalent in the society. The central government as well as State governments are quite conscious for the upliftment of SC, ST and other backward and weaker sections of the society including women.

In pursuance of Articles 330 and 332 of the Constitution, seats are reserved for SC, ST in the parliament and State assemblies in proportion to their population. In government services, 15 per cent are reserved for the SC candidates and this reservation is also to be maintained in the promotion in the services of all groups. Besides, 5 years relaxation in the age is also made for SC candidates. The State governments and union territories administrations have separate departments to look after the welfare of SC and other weaker sections. Apart from the central and State governments, a number of voluntary organisations are also engaged in promoting the welfare of the SC in the country.

For the promotion of education in SC population both the Central and State governments are giving scholarships at various levels for boys and girls belonging to scheduled castes. In the same way, pre-examination coaching centres at centre and State levels have been set up in various parts of the country of preparing the prospective candidates for various competitive examinations.

The study reveals that despite all efforts made by government, social reform agencies and SC of their own, the socio-economic condition of SC population in India is very backward though it has an improving trend. The concept of untouchability is being removed in urban areas while it is in practice to a considerable extent in rural areas of the country. The SC villagers are in the grip of mass illiteracy but now they are beginning to understand the importance of education in their life and have begun to send their children to school. Being illiterate and unskilled, they are bound to work in low-paid and manual activities and services.

In many areas of the country, particularly in rural areas, SC are suppressed by upper castes and they are bound to maintain their traditional occupations and to work in the fields and houses of the upper caste families. In our democratic and welfare State, it is expected that in the near future, SCs will have a status similar to other castes and groups in different fields of life, i.e., social, economic, political, cultural, etc.

NOTES

Bateille, Andre (1992): Society and Politics in India. *Essays in Comparative Perspective*, O.U.P.: Delhi, p. 224.

Census of India (1991): Series 1, Union Primary Census Abstract for Scheduled Castes and Scheduled Tribes.

Garg, S.K. (1981): 'Law and Constitution for Social Change'. In L.R. Singh (ed.): *Nation Building and Development Process*, Rawat Publications: Jaipur and Delhi, p. 206

Gosal, R.P.S. (1991): Work Force of India's Scheduled Caste Population: A Spatial Perspective, *Population Geography*, Vol. 13(143), pp. 7-22.

Gupta, Sharad (1994): Harijan Backward Clashes on the Rise, *Times of India,* Lucknow, Feb. 2, 1994 p. 5

Hidayatulla, M. (1994): Foreword to 'Competing Equalities' by M. Galanter, Oxford University Press, Delhi, 1984.

Jauhari, A. S. (1990): Scheduled Castes and Scheduled Tribes of India : Study of the Dimension of Some of Their Socio-Cultural Problems (ed.). *Scheduled Castes and Scheduled Tribes*, Chugh Publication, Allahabad, pp.1-29.

Kamat, A. R. (1981): Education and Social Change amongst the Scheduled Castes

and Scheduled Tribes, *Economic and Political Weekly,* Vol. 16, No. 31, Aug. 1.
Kumar , A. (1984): 'The Reform Movements for Upliftment of Scheduled Castes' *Avadh Journal of Social Science,* Vol. 1.
Lal, A.K. (1980): 'Educational Problems of the Scheduled Caste Communities of Bihar', *Social Welfare,* Vol. 26 No. 11.
Maurya, S. D. (1989): Socio-economic Structure of Scheduled Caste Population in Uttar Pradesh (ed.). *Population and Housing Problems in India.* Chugh Publication, Allahabad.
Menon, P.S.K. (1993): 'Abolition of Untouchability and Removal of Social Disabilities: An Appraisal,' *Yojana,* Vol. 37, No. 23, Dec. 31, p. 21.
Mukherjee, A.B. (1971): 'Density and Relative Strength of the Scheduled Castes Population in Andhra Pradesh', *Indian Geography,* Vol. 46, pp. 23-29.
Pant, S.K. (1994): Socio-economic Programmes for Scheduled Castes & Scheduled Tribes: A Case for introspection, paper submitted in National Seminar.
Sachchidananda (1974): *Education among the Scheduled Castes and Scheduled Tribes in Bihar*, A.N.S. Institute of Social Studies, Patna.
Sachchidananda (1977): *The Harijan Elite,* Haryana: Thomson Press.
Singh, L.R. (1983): A Diagnostic Survey of Socio-economic Conditions of the Scheduled Castes in Banda District of U.P. Research Project No. 10. G.B. Pant Social Science Institute, Allahabad.
Singh, L.R. (1986): Impact of Development Programmes on Socio-economic Conditions of Scheduled Castes in Rae Bareli District of U.P., Research Project, G.B. Pant Social Science, Institute, Allahabad.
Singh, L.R. and Dina Nath (1981): Spatial Patterns of Rural Scheduled Caste Population in the Saryupar Plain, *Geographical Review of India*, Vol. 43, No. 4.
Singh, Sunit (1995): "Anusuchit Jati Par Atyachar Aparadhiyon Ke Dandit Karne Mein Badhaein" a paper submitted in National Seminar in G.B. Pant Social Science Institute, Allahabad.
Tripathi, Raj Mani (1997): 'Females Participation in Work Force in Uttar Pradesh,' *National Geographer,* Vol. XXXIII, No. 2.

8

SOCIAL TRANSFORMATION AMONG SCHEDULED CASTES IN BIHAR DUE TO JOB RESERVATION

Case Study of Three Generations in Bihar

RAJALAXMI RATH

The policy of compensatory discrimination and the various constitutional provisions aimed at giving preferential treatment to the scheduled castes especially with regard to the provision of reservation of jobs in the public services is unique in nature. Due to the oppression of centuries the scheduled castes have remained backward in all respects and have come to occupy the lowest place in the society. Poverty, illiteracy and unemployment are the major problems facing the communities. Independence ushered in an era of developmental planning wherein greater stress was given both by the administration as well as by voluntary effort to accelerate the pace of all-round development of the poorest sections of the society. This is not possible without ameliorating the socio-economic conditions of this section of the population. The reservations of jobs in public services has given earnings and the security, patronage and prestige to a sizeable portion of the beneficiary group that go with Government service. Hence it continues to be regarded as one of the major instruments of State policy with its declared objective of ushering in a new social order.

The State of Bihar offers a rich area for the study of the effects of this policy. With its sizeable population of scheduled castes, years of under-development, semi-feudal economic conditions, social tensions on grounds of caste and community, the State presents interesting and unique aspects of the process of social change. According to the 1991 census Bihar has a scheduled caste population of 125.72 lakhs, which accounts for 14.55 per cent of the State's total population of 863.74 lakhs. 92 per cent of these scheduled castes live in the rural areas, which is higher than the all-India figure of 84 per cent. In Bihar 23 castes have been scheduled by the Constitution. The dominating among the scheduled castes are Chamar, Dusadh, Pasi, Dhobi and Mushar. But other scheduled castes like Dom, Mehter, Rajwar, Bauri, Turi, Ghasi etc. are still at the bottom of social and economic development due to their extreme backwardness and poverty.

A number of schemes have been included for the benefit of the scheduled castes in the various Five Year Plans. The earlier plans aimed at the general development of all sections of the society. It was believed that the fruits of development would percolate to the economically backward classes or the lowest strata of society. But it was not to be so. It kept on benefiting the better off and in the process the disparity between these communities and the upper strata of the country grew wider. The Sixth Plan therefore made a departure from the earlier plan documents and aimed at the development of the weaker sections or the scheduled castes separately from the general communities. The subsequent plans have made improvements and several beneficiary-oriented, poverty-alleviation programmes have been introduced in order to lend economic support to individual poor families and bring these families above the poverty line in a phased manner.

The present study was undertaken to find out the contrast in the socio-economic conditions of three generations of the respondents namely the parents, the beneficiaries and their children. It is in the nature of an investigation into the effect of the policy of reservation on the process of social transformation. This chapter is outcome of survey conducted on 120 respondents of the scheduled castes and belonging to the Class-I, Class-II, and Class-III services. Respondents have been chosen at three phases of their service career, namely those who had recently joined service, with about 1-10 years of service, those who have put in about 10-20 years of service, as well as those who have reached the fag-end of their career having put in more than 20 years of service. Such grouping was necessary to find out a wide range or reactions to the questionnaire from the different age-groups of service-holders. In Bihar the scheduled castes are found more or less in all regions of the State, hence interviews for the beneficiaries were conducted at almost all districts of the State as well as the State-headquarters. This was imperative in order to take into account any regional variations so that an overall picture of the entire State may emerge. The respondents were selected at random in order to eliminate the possibility of any bias. A questionnaire consisting of a total number of 58 main questions and several sub-questions were devised to elicit information from the beneficiaries. The questionnaire has been devised to cover a wide range of issues concerning the beneficiary himself, his parents, his family, his colleagues and the public. The beneficiaries opinion was sought on vital issues to test the degree of social transformation that he has undergone after joining service.

Constitutional Provisions

The safeguards, which pointedly deal with the reservation of jobs in public services are Article 16 (4), 320 and 335.

Article 16 gives equal opportunity to all citizens in matters relating to employment or appointment to any office under the State without discriminating on grounds of race, caste, sex, descent etc. Clause (4) of Article 16 specifically states that "Nothing in this article shall prevent the State from making any provision for the reservation of appointment to posts in favour of any backward classes of citizens which, in the opinion of the State, is not adequately represented in the services under the State." Article 320 makes it the duty of the Union and State Public Service Commission to conduct examinations for appointments to the services in the Union and States but clause (4) of Article 320 specifies that it shall not be required, for the Public Service Commission to be consulted as respects the manner in which any provision referred to in Clause (4) or Article 16 may be made or as respects the manner in which effect may be given to the provisions of Article 335. Under Article 335 The claims of the members of the scheduled castes and the scheduled tribes shall be taken into consideration, consistently with the maintenance of efficiency of administration, in the making of appointments to services and posts in connections with the affairs of the Union or of State. It is to be noted that the preferential treatment under Article 335 is accorded to members of the scheduled castes and scheduled tribes only, and not to members of backward classes' in general, as does Article 16(4).

As per the constitutional provisions contained in the Articles 16 (4) and 335 the Government of Bihar introduced reservation for scheduled castes on the basis of the percentage of their population. According to the census of 1961 it was fixed at 14 per cent for appointments made directly at the State level. But the percentage of reservation at the divisional and district levels were kept at different levels, which is in proportion to the concentration of scheduled caste population in the particular division or district. Similarly 50 point rosters have been prepared for the divisional and district level. The roster varies from district to district and division to division since percentage of reservation is different depending on the concentration of scheduled caste population. The same is the percentage in the matter of promotion in posts too.

The most striking feature of the 120 service holders in the Class I, Class II, and Class III interviewed is that about 65 per cent have dropped their caste surnames adding secular surnames like 'Prasad', 'Kumar' and 'Ranjan' etc. Whereas, earlier while eliciting information on the father's name of the beneficiary almost all had their caste surnames. In fact this gives a picture of three generations very clearly. The respondent's father had the caste-surname attached to his name. The beneficiary, who is the second generation in line has deleted it to a great extent and in the latter part of the interview the beneficiaries, have themselves admitted the anxiety to delete the caste surname from the names of their children. This is indicative of the desire for social mobility in the same family over three generations.

The degree of social transformation as a consequence of entry into service depends to a large extent on the socio-economic background of the beneficiary since the attitudes and the personality traits are influenced considerably by the family of a person. Relevant queries on the educational status of parents revealed that most of them had no formal education as the spread of education among them is limited. As to their fathers, two-thirds of them were either illiterate or semi-literate, whereas 20 per cent were matriculates or above. Their mothers had no formal education. In contrast each one of the beneficiary in the Class I, Class II and Class III are well educated and were vehement about educating their wards to the utmost of their capacity. The most revealing factor is that with regard to education of their girl child 100 per cent wanted their daughter to be properly educated so that she could take up a job if the necessity arose. The male beneficiaries' own spouses were not all that educated. The survey reveals that above 50 per cent are illiterate and 80 per cent had little or no formal education, only 20 per cent were educated. In spite of this the general outlook of the scheduled castes have undergone a real change and each respondent has voiced the compelling need for imparting education to their girls. They felt that the female literacy among them is pitiably low hence the need. Such radical attitude among the influential sections of these communities is bound to have salutary effects in the process of social change in the communities. This is evident in the comparison of three generations in a family with regard to education. There is a clear indication of the intense desire for social mobility. In the case of the respondents' mothers almost 100 per cent cases had no education worth mentioning, 80 per cent of their spouses had no formal education but their daughters were mostly in good schools and being educated with the aim of being suitable for the job market.

The survey also revealed that all the respondents, had given up their caste-based traditional occupation. Each one had proper education and a job in the public services. Whereas, 37.5 per cent of the respondents' fathers were still practising their traditional occupation, 26.5 per cent were in some private jobs, 36 per cent were in Government jobs but only in the Class III and IV category. But coming to the children of the respondents each one was aspiring for a top job. This just gives an insight into the trend in the last fifty years. It is a positive one and shows that a perceptible dent has been made and reservation of jobs has definitely helped the deprived castes by giving them a share in the job market and the social standing thereof. This survey also reveals that nearly a little above one-third of the respondents belong to families in which the traditional occupation was being pursued and about two-thirds of the respondents were the wards of job-holders whether government or private. This trend shows a clear bias of the benefit of reservation in favour of the wards of service holders. It is obvious that wards of such families have grown up in a more advantageous environment in which they have got better facilities for education and other consequent opportunities like better personality development, self-confidence and better access to employment. On the other hand, most of the aspirants from families engaged in the traditional occupation of their castes have remained deprived of these opportunities and have not therefore been able to compete successfully in the job market in large number. Nevertheless, each one of the beneficiaries was keen to make his ward educationally well equipped in order to compete for the best job. This clearly shows a change in attitude over three generations — from one pursuing the traditional occupation to the second generation with a job and finally the third generation looking forward to the best possible job.

No study can be complete without enquiries into the economic condition of the respondent family. Interview conducted with respect to the ancestral properties like house and land revealed that only 38 and 42 per cent of the parents of the respondents had ancestral house and land respectively whereas with the better economic condition due to a job 74 and 76 per cent of the beneficiarie had acquired house and land respectively in their services career. This shows the substantial change in the economic status of the beneficiaries because of their entry into service and economic benefit thereof. With regard to the third generation or the children of the beneficiaries it is inevitable that by the time of their retirement from service they are bound to own some property which lends credence to the fact that with a job there is a certain improvement in the economic status spreading over three generations in the same family.

Due to the financial benefits of the job there has been improvement in their standard of living, but the level of improvement was more conspicuous among those whose parents had been pursuing their traditional occupation. Those respondents whose parents were already in Government service were more confident, economically better off and had already a better living standard. They, therefore, did not experience much of a change in their life style. Otherwise most of the respondents felt that there was a marked improvement in their standard of living. It was either by way of better food, housing facilities and other amenities, but it definitely showed an improvement in the life-style. The few who did not feel any apparent change in their life-style were the ones who were already well off so they could not feel much change. They had attained horizontal mobility. But one thing is for certain: all the respondents had a chance to free themselves of the caste occupation for good, due to the Government service.

An attempt was made to find out the way the beneficiaries were accepted by their neighbours. This could throw light on the extent of their social acceptability by people outside their caste especially the upper castes. It has been found that majority of these respondents had been accepted in their place of posting, whereas they felt that it was not so in their ancestral village. This acceptance was mostly due to the power and prestige of Government service and consequent migration to urban areas where caste feeling is diminishing fast. Obviously it is due to the security, salary and social standing a job provides. As to the treatment meted out to them by their upper caste colleagues and subordinates a majority felt that they were discriminated against by both their colleagues and subordinates. They felt that it was mostly due to the grudge they bore against them for availing of a reserved post. The beneficiaries were looked upon and treated as usurpers. Only a small section felt that they were treated like equals and given a place of importance by both their upper caste colleagues and subordinates. This was however an indication that a small section of the scheduled castes seemed to have succeeded in gaining some social prestige due to a government job. The government job ensures a higher social status not only for those elites among the scheduled castes but also for their communities. In contrast the beneficiary parents had the stigma of untouchability attached to them. Art. 17 abolished untouchability but the social acceptance cannot come with any legislation. What is important is a change in the attitude of the individuals, vis-a-vis acceptance of each other. But the survey reveals that, the children of the beneficiaries did not face any such problem in their social interactions.

There is enough evidence of social mobility taking place among these communities. The rigidity of the caste-system is so elaborate and deep-rooted that it is not so easy to overhaul the system. Nevertheless, it is found that a perceptible dent in the system has been achieved over the years, which is becoming more and more evident with the passage of time. A contrast of treatment meted out by society to three generations as discussed above makes the point quite clear. In the case of the first generation service-holders among these communities it is generally found that the previous generation had suffered from many discriminations and social disabilities, whereas, the next generation consisting of their children were more acceptable in the general society. In fact, the children of the beneficiaries felt less inhibited and could mix freely with children of all communities. The status of the first generation service-holders is in the nature of a transitional phase from an era of underprivileged position to an era of more secular social communion. There are no doubt some exceptions but by and large this is the general trend emerging in the case of the job holders in these communities.

There is also a growing tendency among the job holders to aspire for upward social mobility through the process of Sanskritisation. Many of them have adopted the Hindu religious practices like worshipping gods and goddesses, celebrating important Hindu festivals and observing certain Hindu rites on the occasion of marriage, birth and death. Most of them hold progressive views on social practices like child-marriage, dowry, small family norm, inter-caste, inter-community marriages and status of women. In fact, many of them are found to be as open minded and cosmopolitan in their outlook as members of any other community. There is a growing sense of self-confidence, determination and social awareness visible among them. The type of visitors a respondent gets is a clear indication of the degree of social change that has occurred. Some decades back it would have been unimaginable for any upper caste Hindu visiting a member of these castes. It is important to note here the extent of social change by these job-holders in just three generations.

It is true that the majority of the respondents feel that they are occupying important positions in the society and enjoying certain amount of power and prestige, which the earlier generation did not. At the same time it is equally true that more than half the respondents also experience a feeling of coldness and estrangement in their relationship vis-a-vis the upper castes. In a way this is the crux of the problem. The State has succeeded to a considerable extent in elevating selected members of the scheduled castes by conferring power and the resultant prestige upon them but their social acceptability has not improved *ipso facto* to the same extent. There appears to be a considerable lag between official and social status of the individual beneficiary. Nevertheless, the State policy of compensatory discrimination has in fact created an impact on the social structure in favour of the depressed classes.

NOTES

Ambedkar, B. R. 1945, *What Congress and Gandhi have done to Untouchables*? Bombay, Thacker and Co.

Bottomore, T.B. 1964, *Elites and Society*, Penguin Books.

Marc, Galanter 1984, *Competing Equalities, Law and Backward Classes in India*, Bombay Oxford University Press.

Rath, Rajalaxmi 1995, *Reservation and Social Transformation among SCs and STs*. New Delhi: Inter-India Publications.

Rath, Rajalaxmi 1996, "Social Implications of Reservation", Concept, Vol. 10 (116-117).

Sachchidananda 1977, *Harijan Elite*. Haryana, Thompson Press.

Sachchidananda 1980, Reservation. *Seminar*, No. 250.

Shah, Ghanshyam 1986, "Protective Discrimination, Equality and Political Will in Reservation" : *Policy Programmes and Issues* edited by V.P. Shah and B.C. Agarwal, Jaipur, Rawat Publications.

Sheth, D.L. 1982, Reservation Policy Revised. *Economic and Political Weekly*, Vol. 22 (46).

9

DALIT LITERACY AND EDUCATION IN BIHAR

JOSE VADASERY

The word '*dalit*' is derived from the Sanskrit root '*dal*'. It means 'to crack open, to rend asunder, to oppress' (Monier Williams, 1872 : 404). Therefore, *dalit* implies 'those who have been broken, ground down by those above them in a deliberate and active way. There is in the word itself an inherent denial of pollution, *karma* and justified hierarchy' (Zelliot, 1978 : 77). As *Dalit Voice* writes, '*dalit* became the only name which the Untouchables of India gave unto ourselves. This name is not only widely accepted now but more than that, it conveys our anger, our determination besides striking a terror in our enemy hearts' (*Dalit Voice*, July 16-31, 1992). In this article '*dalit*' refers to the so-called 'ex-Untouchables' whom Gandhi called as 'Harijans' and the Indian Constitution refers to as Scheduled Castes. So I use '*dalit*' and 'Scheduled Castes' as convertible terms.

The general literacy rate of Bihar is 38.48 per cent (male 52 per cent and female 23 per cent) as against India's 52.11 per cent (male 64 per cent and female 39 per cent). The national literacy rate of the Scheduled Castes is 37.41 per cent (male 49.91 per cent and female 23.76 per cent). In Bihar the literacy rate of the Scheduled Caste population is 15.12 per cent (Male 23.97 per cent and female 5.44 per cent). This implies that 76.03 per cent of males and 94.56 per cent of females among the Scheduled Castes are illiterate. (Table 9.1)

The gap in literacy rates between the Scheduled Castes at the national level and the Scheduled Castes at the State level is too glaring. In the case of female literacy (Scheduled Castes) the national average is nearly

Table 9.1: Literacy Rates of Scheduled Castes (India and Bihar) 1961 - 1991

India				Bihar		
Persons	*Male*	*Female*	*Year*	*Persons*	*Male*	*Femal*
10.27	16.96	3.29	1961	5.95	11.2	0.9
(24.0)	(34.5)	(13.0)		(18.4)	(29.8)	(6.9)
14.67	22.36	6.44	1971	6.53	11.9	1.00
(29.5)	(39.5)	(18.7)		(19.94)	(30.64)	(8.72)
21.38	31.12	10.93	1981	10.40	18.02	2.51
(36.2)	(46.9)	(24.8)		(26.20)	(38.11)	(13.62
37.41	49.91	23.76	1991	15.12	23.97	5.44
(52.11)	(64)	(39)		(38.48)	(52.00)	(23)

Note: The general Literacy Rate is given in brackets.

five times more than that of the State of Bihar. In the same way the Scheduled Castes' literacy rate of Bihar is less than half of that of the country. In fact, among the States, Bihar has the lowest literacy rate among the Scheduled Castes. (Table 9.2)

Table 9.2: The Scheduled Castes Literacy Rate (Bihar) Male & Female, Rural & Urban

Year	*Total*	*Male*	*Rural*	*Urban*	*Female*	*Rural*	*Urban*
1981	10.40	18.02	16.28	24.27	2.51	1.78	10.83
1991	15.12	23.97	22.06	42.47	5.44	4.25	17.82

In Bihar the difference in literacy rate among the Scheduled Castes between the rural and urban is similar to that of the State of Bihar and that of the Union. The gap between the rural and urban literacy rates has widened considerably during the last decade. The difference between the rural and urban male literacy rate in 1981 was 8 per cent and it galloped to more than 20 per cent in 1991. The male literacy rate of Bihar is almost five times more than the female literacy rate. (Table 9.3)

Table 9.3: Districts with the Highest and the Lowest Literacy Rates of Scheduled Castes

Highest		*Lowest*	
East Singhbhum	34.51 (23.23)	Araria	8.03 (2.59)
Ranchi	27.45 (15.69)	Sitamarhi	8.51 (1.60)
West Singhbhum	27.18 (14.56)	Saharsa	8.68 (2.49)
Dhanbad	26.34 (11.69)	Madhepura	9.57 (2.47)
Lohardaga	25.87 (14.10)	Purnea	9.80 (3.95)
Patna	23.74 (10.95)	West Champaran	10.19 (2.46)
Gumla	21.47 (11.30)	East Champaran	10.35 (2.78)

Note: Female Literacy Rate is given in brackets.

There is glaring disparity in literacy rate based on the geographical placement of the Scheduled Caste communities. As one moves from South Bihar to North Bihar there is a significant and steady decline in literacy rate. The highest literacy rate among the Scheduled Castes is recorded in the tribal belt of Chhota Nagpur. The districts in Central Bihar have largely medium level literacy rate whereas the districts in North Bihar commonly present low level of literacy rate among the Scheduled Castes.

Districts in Bhojpur area have higher literacy rate among the Scheduled Castes compared to those in North Bihar, (Bhojpur—19.76, Rohtas—20.20, Aurangabad—17.72). The districts of Saran, Siwan and Gopalgunj also have similar trend having 18.63, 17.87 and 15.68 per cent of literacy respectively.

The same phenomenon is noticed with regard to the female literacy rate. The lowest literacy rate among women is recorded in North Bihar. The district of Sitamarhi presents a very dismal picture of having just 1.60 per cent of literacy among *dalit* women. This indicates that almost the entire *dalit* female population of the district is illiterate. Whereas the district of Singhbhum has 23.23 per cent of female literacy. No serious study has been conducted to find out what makes certain districts to have high female literacy while other districts lag behind. (Table 9.4)

Table 9.4: Districts with the Highest and the Lowest Rural Female Illiteracy Rates of Scheduled Castes

	Highest		*Lowest*	
No.	*Districts*	*Illiteracy*	*Districts*	*Illiteracy*
1	Sitamarhi	98.66	East Singhbhum	84.73
2.	West Champaran	98.10	Lohardaga	87.58
3.	Madhubani	98.02	West Singhbhum	88.86
4.	Madhepura	97.87	Ranchi	89.37
5.	Araria	97.74	Gumla	89.67
6.	Darbhanga	97.49	Sahibgunj	93.87

Disparity in literacy is noticed among the various castes of the Scheduled Castes. The rate of literacy is high in castes which are numerically small like Dabgar (15.64 per cent), Sawansi (15.27), Lalbegi (14.23), Halalkhor (10.39), etc. Among the populous communities like Ravidasis (7.03), Dussadhs (7.97) and Musahars (1.31) the percentage of literacy is rather low. However, Dhobis (11.95), Pasis (11.71) and Mehtars (10.15) have high literacy rate in comparison with many other

Scheduled Castes. The Musahars (1.31) and the Bhuiyas (1.54) have the lowest literacy rate among the Scheduled Castes (Census 1971). The fact that some castes predominate and others are under-represented suggests an uneven growth of education among the several castes of Scheduled Castes. The trend continues as the following data indicates. (Table 9.5)

Table 9.5: Growth in Literacy Rate of the Scheduled Castes—A Comparative Study

Caste	*1971*	*1981*	*Caste*	*1971*	*1981*	*Caste*	*1971*	*1981*
Ravidasi	7.03	11.52	Dabgar	15.61	22.28	Musahar	1.31	2.20
Dussadh	7.97	12.43	Pan/Sawansi	15.27	27.05	Bhuiya	1.54	4.30
Dhobi	11.95	18.56	Lalbegi	14.23	18.24			
Pasi	11.71	17.58	Halalkhor	10.39	19.38			

However, studies conducted in other States suggest that castes that constitute a large percentage of the Scheduled Caste population generally predominate in literacy like the Mahars of Maharashtra, the Malas and Madiyas of Andhra Pradesh, the Ravidasis of U.P., the Pulayas of Kerala, the Ad Dharmis of Punjab, etc.

In Bihar Ravidasis and Dussadhs are considered as the most important Scheduled Caste communities and have thrown up important political leaders but even among them the bulk of the community members are not out of the illiteracy net (Sachchidananda, 1997 : 170). However, on account of the numerical strength of the above two castes the benefits of the government facilities mostly go to them. A random survey conducted among the Scheduled Caste students in Bihar by the ICSSR shows that among the high school students Ravidasis constituted 34.5 per cent, Dussadhs 26.43 per cent, Pasis 17.8 per cent, Dhobis 13.8 per cent, Musahars 0.58 per cent and the rest 6.8 per cent. The same survey among the college students shows that Ravidasis constituted 38.22 per cent, Dussadhs 36.44 per cent, Pasis 8 per cent, Dhobis 12.89 per cent, Musahars 0.44 per cent and the rest 4.04 per cent (Vimal P. Shah, 1982).

This shows that more than 60 per cent of the High School students and 75 per cent of the College students of the Scheduled Castes belong to the two numerically strong castes of Ravidas and Dussadh. Although the government facilities for the education of the Scheduled Castes have succeeded in drawing the Scheduled Caste children from illiterate homes or rural occupation background the benefits of the facilities are not evenly distributed. The worst affected group in Bihar is the Musahars who in spite of being the third largest Scheduled Caste community in the State have meagre representation of 0.58 and 0.44 per cent High School and College students among the Scheduled Caste students of Bihar. One has to be educated to get the benefits of government facilities. The sociologists and educationists have treated the *dalits* as one social entity whereas they are heterogeneous. There are considerable social, cultural and economic differences among the *dalits* based on their origin and status in the caste hierarchy. A meaningful education policy for the *dalits* need to take into account these internal differences among the *dalits*. (Table 9.6).

Table 9.6: Percentage of SC & ST Students in Bihar

	I-V	*VI-VIII*	*IX-X*	*XI-XII*
SC	15.65	10.02	7.97	10.26
ST	8.96	6.71	5.80	3.68

Source: School Education Profile, 1993.

The female literacy rate of the Scheduled Castes in Bihar (5.44 per cent) is considered to be the lowest in the country. The national sample survey of the ICSSR of the Scheduled Caste boys and girls shows that only 15 per cent of the Scheduled Caste High School students and 10 per cent of the College students are girls. "The marginally higher representation of girls in the school sample as compared to the college sample supports the recurrent observation that the representation of females in education declines progressively at successively higher levels of education" (Suma Chitnis, 1981:15). The following data shows that the girls representation at all stages of education is much lower than that of the boys. The boys are 2.2 times more than the girls in the primary school, 2.05 in the middle school, 4.28 in the high school, 9.9 at the graduation (arts) and 9.11 (Science), 21.7 in Commerce, 22.9 in B.Eng. It also shows that in specialised studies the *dalits* are inclined to join polytechnic, ITI and Arts and Crafts. In Science and Commerce they are poorly represented (Table 9.7).

Problems of Dalit Education

Dropout and stagnation are among the major problems of the education of the Scheduled Caste children. More than 60 per cent from among those who enter the first standard dropout before they reach the fourth

Table 9.7: Number of S.C. Students (Bihar) studying at Various Stages during the Year 1995-1996

Stages	*Boys*	*Girls*	*Total*
Pre-Primary	700(6.83)	540 (5.60)	1240 (6.24)
Primary (I-V)	934509 (15.90)	431483 (9.25)	1365992 (15.02)
Middle (VI-VIII)	194108 (11.65)	65584 (9.25)	259692 (19.94)
High School (IX-X)	72016 (9.90)	16840 (6.90)	88856 (9.14)
Intermediate	5959 (11.81)	2124 (11.17)	8083 (11.63)
B.A.	10899 (7.81)	1104 (2.78)	12003 (6.69)
B.Sc.	2605 (4.72)	286 (3.64)	2891 (4.59)
B.Com.	1391 (0.70)	64 (0.14)	1455 (0.60)
B.E.(Eng.)	275 (4.62)	12 (3.63)	287 (4.57)
MBBS, Ayurveda	1085 (8.63)	205 (13.02)	1290 (9.14)
BEd, BT	142 (10.26)	47 (5.21)	189 (8.40)
MA	548 (6.90)	93 (3.32)	641 (5.97)
M.Sc.	63 (2.78)	21 (3.67)	84 (2.96)
B.Com	41 (0.37)	15 (0.44)	56 (0.39)
Ph.D.	34 (5.64)	25 (16.55)	59 (7.83)
TTC	114 (6.73)	49 (5.96)	163 (6.48)
Polytechnic	554 (14.07)	12 (8.63)	566 (13.88)
ITI/ Arts & Crafts	1539 (15.03)	82 (8.96)	1621 (14.53)

Notes: 1. The figures given in brackets indicate the percentage of SC students to the corresponding total enrolment.

2. Table compiled by PSC on the data, supplied by Ministry of HRD (Department of Education) Govt. of India.

standard. As many as 80 per cent dropout before they complete the High School education. Human Resource Development Ministry in its report (1993) says that the highest percentage of dropout in the primary section is from the SC/ST communities. According to the report 79.88 per cent of the SC and 86.72 per cent of the ST students dropout in the primary level. The situation in Bihar is rather deplorable. The Sixth all-India Educational Survey jointly conducted in 1993 by the Bihar State Education Survey Unit and the National Informatics Centre, Planning Commission, Government of India gives the following data (Table 9.9).

The data shows that among the Scheduled Caste students enrolled in class I, 15.53 per cent complete VIIIth class and 5.42 per cent complete their matric and only 1.22 per cent complete their intermediate. The data also shows that less than 1 per cent of *dalit* girls enrolled in class I complete their plus two.

In the same way the problem of stagnation, viz, the phenomenon of repetition of school and college years is either due to failure in examination and the consequent denial of promotion to the next class or

Table 9.8: Number of Scheduled Caste Students Studying at Various Stages during the Year 1995-1996 at the National Level

Stages	*Boys*	*Girls*	*Total*	*Per cent Bihar dalits*
Pre-Primary	108658 (9.38)	93322 (9.51)	201980 (9.44)	0.61
Primary (I-V)	10935830 (17.53)	7601593 (16.04)	18537423 (16.89)	7.37
Middle (VI-VIII)	3700922 (14.82)	2152901 (13.41)	5853823 (14.27)	4.44
High School (IX-X)	14724226 (13.76)	656787 (10.82)	2129213 (12.68)	4.17
Intermediate	879257 (16.29)	338439 (12.47)	1217696 (15.01)	0.66
B.A.	47794 (7.54)	73864 (7.25)	273568 (11.23)	4.39
B.Sc.	44833 (5.65)	22491 (6.48)	70285 (7.19)	4.11
B.Com.	17492 (6.43)	15251 (4.62)	600084 (5.35)	0.24
B.E. (Eng.)	17492 (6.43)	3592 (7.95)	21084 (6.64)	1.36
MBBS, Ayurveda	6391 (8.83)	3570 (9.36)	9961 (9.01)	12.95
B.Ed. B.T.	8902 (12.39)	3633 (7.22)	12535 (10.26)	1.51
M.A.	28695 (17.40)	767 (0.73)	36302 (13.47)	1.76
M.Sc.	5212 (8.24)	1854 (5.18)	7066 (7.13)	1.19
M.Com.	4760 (7.85)	1227 (6.67)	5987 (7.57)	0.94
Ph.D.	1158 (3.87)	356 (3.10)	1514 (3.66)	3.87
TTC	14816 (25.34)	6336 (11.52)	21152 (18.64)	0.77
Polytechnic	30877 (11.64)	5515 (9.97)	36392 (11.35)	1.56
ITI, Arts & Crafts	44414 (12.59)	8418 (14.53)	52832 (12.86)	3.07

Note: The figures in brackets indicate the percentage of SC students to the corresponding total enrolment.

Source: Table compiled by PSC on the data supplied by Ministry of H.R.D., (Dept. of Education), Govt. of India (Excluding the data 'Per cent—Bihar *dalits*').

Table 9.9: The Dropout Rate of SC & ST Students in Bihar

	I-VIII	*VIII-X*	*X-XII*
S.C.	84.47	94.58	98.78
S.C. Girls	89.05	97.18	99.01
S.T.	81.21	93.10	99.24
S.T. Girls	84.32	94.72	99.37

due to gaps and breaks in school or college attendance necessitated by economic difficulties, poor health or other problems. The incidence of stagnation, like the incidence of dropout, is considered to be far more acute among the Scheduled Caste students than among others, (*ibid.*, 38).

The incentives provided by the Union and State governments have very limited role in helping the overwhelmingly large majority of the *dalits* living under conditions of staggering poverty to go in for education. Human Resource Development Ministry's report (1993) shows that even the free mid-day meal scheme of the government introduced in seventeen Indian States to attract the students from the poor sections to schools has not really affected the dropouts. According to the report the free mid-day meal has no real impact on the SC/ST communities.

Problems like dropout, stagnation and failure in competitive examinations lead to further inferiorization of the *dalits*. The dominant castes especially in the rural areas are generally contemptuous of the education of *dalit* children. They have their own vested interest in keeping the *dalits* illiterate. The same attitude is reflected among the teachers especially of the dominant castes who are entrusted with the job of teaching the *dalit* children. It is reported from Rohtas Block, "Harijan children are not allowed to join schools and if they are being admitted, they are not allowed to sit together with the children of caste Hindus" (Prasad, Varma and Thakur, 1987 : 47). The same report says, "In Madhubani, Harijans are not allowed to utilize the bathing ghats, tea stalls, public temples used by the caste Hindus. The study shows that social disability of Harijans in the area is regarded customary by caste Hindus particularly high caste Brahmins and the Harijans are forced to lead a sub-human life. Sometimes they are beaten up by the high caste people." Another study on the Musahars of Bhojpur and Darbhanga districts also reveals the same phenomenon. It says, "In most of the cases Musahars are not allowed to sit in the presence of dominant caste people even on a separate cot or 'chouki'. This practice is observed relatively more strictly in the Bhojpur area.... It is found that majority of the respondents are discriminated in the use of public conveniences mainly by the dominant castes of the respective sampled areas, more or less similarly. Their pollution is considered so contagious that mere touching of a hand pump of the employer can cause anger to the landlords" (Tiwary, S.N., 1989). There exists a nexus between the dominant castes and the teachers to keep the *dalit* students out of education. The social environment considerably affects the interests of the *dalits* in education. (Table 9.10).

Table 9.10: Percentage of Teachers on the Basis of Caste and Sex

SC	*ST*	*OBC*	*Female*
7.50	7.27	27.72	19.75

Source: School Education Profile, 1993.

Among the teachers in Bihar the total female representation is less than 20 per cent presenting a deplorable situation. This has its negative impact on the education of girls. In the same way the data shows that the Scheduled Castes, Scheduled Tribes, and Backward Castes are poorly represented.

Dr. S.P. Jain, in his article 'Backward Classes: Problems of Education', says that the school-college level curriculum chiefly in subjects like languages, civics, history, etc. should be proportionately balanced representing the concerns and aspirations of different sections of students. But in reality they represent the interests of the dominant social groups. The *dalits* and the tribals hardly get a token representation in the curriculum. A recent study of the Hindi readers published by the NCERT and of the Madhya Pradesh Text Book Corporation for classes four, five and six brings out clearly the gap between the curricular representation of knowledge and the lives of *dalits* and the tribals. Of the seventy-seven story lessons, the study surmise, only two had central characters identifiable as a tribal and none had a *dalit* as a central character. The two communities comprise one-third of the State's population (Jain, 1988).

"If the material of these books is taken as the microcosm of the State's society, then the SC and ST are the people nearly invisible in this microcosm. Also, if the pursuits and experiences of the non-SC/ST included in these books are considered symbols of knowledge, then by implication, the pursuits and experiences of the SC/ST stand rejected as symbols of ignorance. The choice for these communities, therefore, remains both disconcerting and difficult. For if their children successfully pursue such a lopsided educational programme they alienate themselves from their moorings. And if they fail or refuse to pursue successfully, they are dismissed as backward or reactionary" (*ibid.*). It is argued that one of the major reasons for the alienation of the *dalit* illiterate from the masses is the content of the curriculum. Education has led to the emergence of a *dalit* elite class which has distanced itself from *dalit* masses and also from *dalit* agitation programmes.

The National Policy of Education (1986) after modification in 1992 says, "To promote equality, it will be necessary to provide equal opportunity to all not only in access, but also in the conditions for success. Besides, awareness of the inherent equality of all will be created through the core curriculum. The purpose is to remove prejudices and complexes transmitted through the social environment and the accident of birth." However, no significant steps have been taken till today to provide a curriculum that is supportive of the *dalit*-tribal needs.

It is also a fact that *dalits* tend to enrol at institutions that have a lower level of performance on account of their economic constraints. The policy makers and administrators do not seem to be interested in providing quality education to the *dalits*. The Bihar Harijan Adivasi Students Union in one of its documents says, "The children of elite families study in convent schools while the children of poor families are pushed into *Charvaha* and *Pahalwan* schools. The government schools in the villages exist without any facilities and the conditions of the 'welfare hostels' (Harijan hostels) are deplorable. The deliberate neglect of the government schools and the welfare hostels is part of a larger conspiracy to keep the poor forever in poverty" (BHASU, 1993). The report also says that the present education system is hostile to the tribal-*dalit* students. Therefore, most of the *dalit* organisations in the State including BHASU demand uniform education policy. The dual education system is one of the major hindrances in promoting *dalit* literacy and education in the State. The curriculum, fee structure and the orientation of public schools, popularly known as 'convent schools', are highly in favour of the rich and upper castes and keep *dalits* out of the ambit of good education.

The terms of new discourse on education system are liberalisation and privatization of education as alternatives to the problems of financing education especially higher education. In this scheme of education the tribals, *dalits* and the weaker sections of the society will have no possibility of getting good education.

Conclusion

The Constitution of India, Article 46 states, "The State shall promote with special care the educational and economic interests of the weaker sections of the people, and, in particular, of the Scheduled Castes and the Scheduled Tribes, and shall protect them from social injustice and all forms of oppression". Article 45 of the Constitution is a 'Directive Principle of State Policy which envisages to provide free and compulsory education to all children until they complete the age of 14 years within a period of 10 years from the commencement of the Constitution. India has completed 50 years of its independence. At this juncture the emerging profile of *dalit* literacy and education in the State of Bihar is as follows:

(a) 85 per cent of the *dalits* in Bihar are illiterate and 94 per cent of our *dalit* women are deprived of literacy.
(b) There are several districts in Bihar where almost the entire *dalit* women are illiterate.
(c) The dropout rate of *dalit* students is very high. Only 5 per cent of them reach up to the Matric.
(d) Studies indicate that untouchability is prevalent in the State. There are villages in Bihar where *dalit* children are not allowed to join schools and if they are being admitted they are not allowed to sit with the children of caste Hindus.
(e) The dual education policy of the government automatically debars the *dalit* students from getting good education. They are forced to be content with ill-equipped government schools including '*Charvaha* and *Pahalwan*' schools, and non-formal education system.
(f) The educational process continues to be governed by the cultural hegemony of the elite classes which are drawn mostly from upper castes.

It is unfortunate that debates on *dalit* education by social scientists, political leaders and others are often limited to the question of effective implementation of reservation policy in education. Though discussions on effective implementation of reservation policy are important, greater stress needs to be laid on creating *dalit* friendly curriculum, providing *dalit* friendly atmosphere in the school campus, eliminating the negative impact of the dual education policy on *dalits* either by controlling the spread of elite educational institutions or by introducing reservation for *dalits* in all private educational institutions, etc. A radical re-thinking on the dual education policy, the content of the curriculum, etc. from the perspective of the *dalits* and tribals is imperative. Dr. Ambedkar says, "The problem of the lower order is to remove from them that inferiority complex which has stunted their growth and made them slaves to others, to create in them the consciousness of the significance of their lives for themselves and for the country, of which they have been cruelly robbed of by the existing social order. Nothing can achieve this purpose except the spread of higher education" (quoted in Silver Jubilee Souvenir of the People's Education Society, Bombay, January 1974).

NOTES

Ambedkar (Quoted in Silver Jubilee Souvenir of the People's Education Society, Bombay), 14th January, 1974.

Anirudh Prasad, Rajan Varma, and Anil K. Thakur (1987) 'Social Disabilities of the Harijans in Bihar' (Report No. XVIII), ANS Institute of Social Studies, Patna.

Annual Report, 1993, Department of Education, Min. of HRD, Govt. of India.

BHASU—'Statement of the Fourth State conference', October 13-15, 1993.

Dalit Voice, July 16-31, 1992.

Jain, S.P. (1988) 'Backward Classes: Problems of Education' in *Times of India* (Patna), July 13,1988.

Monier-Williams (1872) *A Sanskrit-English Dictionary*, Oxford, Clarendon Press.

National Policy on Education—1986 (with modifications undertaken in 1992), Deptt. of Education, Ministry of HRD, Govt. of India.

Sachchidananda (1997) 'The Harijans of Bihar' in *Social Realities in Bihar* (ed.) Sachchidananda, K.K. Varma, Manohar Lal; Novelty & Co. Patna.

Statistical data is based on 1991 Census unless otherwise mentioned.

Suma Chitnis (1981) 'A Long Way to Go—A Report on a Survey of Scheduled Castes High School and College Students in Fifteen States in India', ICSSR, Allied Publishers, Delhi.

Tiwary, S.N. (1989) 'Sociology of Poverty: A Study of the Musahars in Rural Darbhanga and Bhojpur Districts' in *ICSSR*, Vol. XVII, January-June, 1989.

Vimal P. Shah (1982) 'The Educational Problems of Scheduled Castes and Scheduled Tribes', *School and College Students in India (A Statistical Profile)*, ICSSR, Allied Publishers, Delhi.

Zelliot Eleanor (1978) 'Dalit—New Cultural context for an old Marathi word' in *Asian Studies.*

10

THE WOMEN'S RESERVATION BILL
Opportunities and Challenges

ARUNDHUTI ROY CHOUDHURY

The Constitution of India has provided for various policy outlines that aim at social upliftment of the weaker sections of society. One of them is that of positive discrimination. The policy involves a conscious act on the part of the State on the basis of some ascriptive criteria such as caste, gender, ethnicity and even spatial location. Different expressions are used to signify the policy, for instance, protective discrimination, reservation, reverse discrimination, positive/affirmative action, preferential treatment, etc.

These provisions together form the framework for the analysis of the concept of social justice in the Indian context. It aims at the reduction of persistent discrimination or inequality in society by giving preferential treatment to the backward/marginalised sections in the distribution of valued social goods and opportunities. It is seen as a means of protecting the weaker sections of society who have for centuries been socially and historically ostracized. It is basically to free the disadvantaged sections from the hegemony of the powerful by creating ample opportunity for their participation. A careful reading of the various constitutional provisions, the policies, the programmes of the government and the target groups or beneficiaries, enables us to identify two types of injustices that our Constitution recognises. This can in general be termed as cultural and economic injustices.

In other words, the policy of reservation or positive discrimination stands, at least in the short run, as an integral part of the process of socio-economic change and development in India. This is clearly provided in the Constitution viz. Articles 15(4), 16(4), 46 and 340. The State is empowered to take special measures for the betterment of the deprived sections of society. It is in line with this provision that the demand for reservation for women in the Parliament is made by a section of the women's movement today.

However, any legal or constitutional measures like reservation to undo social discrimination and injustice more often than not becomes a subject of controversy. Similarly, the public discourse on political quotas for women in the parliament is marked with much debate in different circles—academics, politicians and the social activists. One of the central issues of debate being why there should be reservation for women, to having caste and community based reservation within the women's reserved seats (beyond those of SC and ST). The debate brings to surface the complex/multiple nature of women's discrimination in Indian society and its related dilemmas. The paper would argue that despite its problematic character, women's movements cannot give up the language of reservation to articulate their rights. Yet, the rapid proliferation of entirely unpredictable forces and the new dynamics may require them to rethink some of the components of the reservation policy by placing it within the concept of contextual social justice.

Within this larger framework of understanding the article is divided into three parts to understand the implication of this measure on the empowerment of women. First, it delves into the major points of the ongoing debate on the policy by the various sections of society. Secondly, it provides substantive facts to uphold the reservation policy given the social set-up in the country. Finally, it argues for transcending the limits of the policy and going for a full, not limited, empowerment of all the oppressed people through an integration of their interest in the reservation policy.

Debate on the Policy

The public debate over reservation for women in Parliament, with some shades of variation, has crystallized into recognisable arguments for and against. The pro-reservation group feel that affirmative action is mandatory for the social upliftment of women. According to them reservation for women as a unified category would help in breaking the existing structures of patriarchy that the present system is intensifying. In their understanding, through reservation women would get politically liberated and come to play a central role in the Indian developmental process. Speaking against the caste-based women's reservation, they point out the anti-women attitudes of the OBCs. There is an underlying assumption that if women become a part of the existing political system, caste discrimination along with patriarchy will weaken automatically. In other words, not only is a straightforward link posited between the presence of women in Parliament and gender justice but also gender is taken as a homogeneous category.

Others are worried that the wrong people would reap benefit from such a provision. That it would only help in broadening the elite base of the existing political structure. Political gamesmanship with reservation will lead to economically dominant castes and creamy layer grabbing the lion's share of benefits, while the truly oppressed and marginalised will continue to be kept out.

They also hold the opinion that within the existing patriarchal gender relations, women will be nothing but puppets in the power plays of upper caste men and political vested interest. Far from promoting gender equality, women's status within the family and community will at best remain unchanged, and at worst, new forms of control and oppression of women will emerge. Based on their experience of reservation in Panchayats in some parts of the country, they argued that reservation has not been proved to be favourable—relatives of established male leaders are fielded, and there is no impact at all on inefficiency and corruption. In other words, rather than levelling the playing field, reservation has widened the gap between women and has consequently failed to bring about social transition.

While there may be fragments of truth arrayed on both sides, the whole truth remains elusive. The situation is much more complex and paradoxical than it appears. And this is mainly due to the fact that women carry the burden of double discrimination. One as being a woman in general and second as belonging to a particular caste or class. In other words, gender is not a homogeneous category. Undoubtedly, patriarchal values run through class, caste and community. Yet it not only differs in form, nature and intensity, but also gender relations are mediated through caste hierarchy. Thus, while women foreground their identity as women to liberate themselves they still have to be equally concerned of their identities as a member of a caste, class, religion, community, etc.

At the same time questions such as: whether community or caste guard's women's rights/interest; will the caste-class-ridden patriarchal communities provide space for them; can lower caste groups constitute alternatives to upper caste domination where women are concerned, remain to be answered (Krishnaraj 1998: 394). Otherwise the *dalit* women may end up being doubly deserted and discriminated.

The Position of Women in the Political Sphere

In order to understand the issue let us for the time being look at the position of women in the political sphere. An analysis of women's participation in elections brings forth a grim situation. Over the past four decades only 36 MPs of the Lok Sabha were women. The average for all our State legislatures is 5 to 7 per cent and so is the all-India average. The highest representation that women have ever enjoyed has been 8 per cent in the Lok Sabha, 15 per cent in the Rajya Sabha, about 11 per cent in the legislative assemblies and 13 per cent in the council of ministers. The average percentage of women between 1952-96 for the Lok Sabha has been 6.0, for the Rajya Sabha 10.3 and 4.0 for the State Assemblies (Seminar, September 1997, p. 50). The picture becomes even more grim when one tries to find the percentage of *dalit* women among them.

Again the same state of affairs is visible in the composition of the political parties. Historically, the political parties have never felt very comfortable with bills related to social and gender justice. Undoubtedly, there has never been any dearth in symbolic gestures, but they have remained in the realm of symbolism only. There are very few instances of concrete initiatives. Thereby, reflecting a wide divergence between what they profess, specially in their manifestoes and practice when in power.

The hypocrisy of the political parties emerges from the fact that, despite their professed commitment to provide one-third representation to women, they ignore this principle while issuing tickets to candidates. And despite their concern for the backward and minority women, most of the women candidates belong to upper caste and class, with a few exceptions (Roy Choudhury 1998).

This emerges clearly when we look at the statistics available of women contestants in Lok Sabha elections. From 1952 to 1996 we find that the average of women contestants per seat was just 0.30 with the average share of women among all the contestants a meagre 3.2 per cent. When one looks at the same figures in the State assemblies from 1952 to 1997 the average of women contestants per seat was as low as 0.19 and the share of women among all contestants only 2.8 per cent, the situation in the State assemblies thus being worse than that in the Lok Sabha.

In the 1996 Lok Sabha elections the BJP put up only 22 female candidates out of which 13 won, i.e., 59 per cent. The number of men candidates fielded was 453 out of which 147 won, i.e., 32.6 per cent. The Congress fielded the maximum number of women candidates, i.e., 50 out of which 16 won, i.e. 32 per cent whereas out of 479 male candidates fielded only 130 won, i.e., 20 per cent. The Janata Dal fielded only 19 women candidates out of which 3 won, i.e., 30 per cent whereas out of 193 male candidates chosen to fight the elections only 40 won, i.e., 20.7 per cent. In other words, women have greater chances of winning the elections. Yet the political parties do not field even 33 per cent of women candidates during elections, leave alone 50 per cent, which is their rightful due (Singhavi 1997:26).

It is equally pertinent to note that even in the supposedly progressive and gender-sensitive left parties in the politbureau of the Communist Party of India-Marxist there were, in 1996, 15 members which included no women. Its central committee had 70 members including five women members, i.e. 7 per cent representation of women. The secretariat of the Communist Party of India had nine members with again no woman member. The Janata Dal political affairs committee had 15 members with no women members. Its parliamentary board had 15 members with again no women included in them. The national executive of the JD had 75 members of which 11 were women, i.e., 15 per cent representation.

From the data available it is clear that the constitutional guarantee for women's equality and also the provision of affirmative action has not got translated significantly into action in all these years of India's independence. The position of women in the political sphere in India is dismal and it becomes worse when one looks at it from the point of view of lower caste women.

The essence of the dismal condition of women and specially that of the marginalised women lies in the existing political and social system of the country. The Indian society is marked by institutionalised gender and caste inequalities. And most of the sitting male MPs and MLAs come from a social milieu which does not question these unequal gender and caste relations. Moreover, politics is no longer about controlling a space in the public domain but more about privatising parts of the public space itself. As a result, it has led to the building of local networks of power and patronage which help the existing male-dominated political parties to win elections. It is basically within this social and political context that one has to locate the concept of positive discrimination and the policy of reservation for women. In this context, how best can one address the issue of reservation for women?.

The Concept of Positive Discrimination and Women

For understanding the purpose of positive discrimination, it is mandatory that we distinguish the concept of social justice from general theory of justice. A general theory of justice as a discourse aims at the whole society, independent of the existing social and power relations of a particular society. It tends to assume a point of view outside the social context where issues of justice arise, in order to gain a comprehensive view. Thus the general theory of justice that claims universality may not always prove to be helpful to analyse socio-cultural specific policies like reverse discrimination.

Social justice, in contrast, derives its principles from a given socio-cultural specificity. It contains some substantive premises about social life, which are usually derived, explicitly or implicitly, from the actual social context in which theorisation takes place. In other words, rights need to be seen as context-dependent even when considered as historically-specific phenomenon (Deshpande 1998: PE-11).

Therefore, social justice as a concept need not always conform to general theory of justice. Since it is socio-culturally specific, it often comes into conflict with the principle of general theory of justice. The theory of social justice cannot be as self-consistent and cohesive as the general theory of justice, mainly because of its dependency on the socio-cultural context from which it emanates. Inconsistency and ambiguity of the concept of social justice is directly proportionate to the complexity of the given socio-economic structure (Sadananda1998: 133-144). Moreover, the fact that the concept of social justice does not arise in a vacuum, it is bound to come into conflict with the already existing power structure.

The Relevance of Women's Reservation

The relevance of the women's reservation has to be located within the basic concept of social justice. In the light of the factual position of women in the political, economic and social sphere, one cannot say that a reform measure like the proposed bill in legislature involves the showering of benefits to an already privileged section of society. In fact, there is no justification to completely terminate the demand for women's reservation in the Parliament.

The transformation of a largely formal democracy which we have today into a substantive democracy with social, economic and political justice made real in our day-to-day life is a task before us. In this context, the policy of reservation may not be a panacea, or even a prerequisite, but nonetheless an important and necessary enabling condition for women's empowerment. It legitimises and provides State sanctions for women's presence in the political sphere, and thereby sends out a larger social message heralding a significant shift in one area of gender power relations.

The women's reservation bill has the potentiality to result in major modifications in the existing power structure, particularly at the constituency level. Further, it would help in breaking the patriarchal value framework, the main plank of which is that women are subordinate to men. Moreover, till date the participation of a handful of women could easily be limited to "soft portfolios" like Health, Education, Social Welfare, Women and Development, etc. Without denigrating the importance of these sectors, a large number of women representatives in Parliament would invariably bring gender at the centre stage of the national developmental process.

Women in the panchayats is an example of this. In a society where there is a tacit consent among women to patriarchy, the panchayati raj results are encouraging. There are cases where women have become a subject of manipulation by local power-brokers or family members but at the same time there are instances where after an initial learning phase, women have taken full control of the system. In fact, today's, women of the panchayats could be tomorrows women representatives in Parliament. In other words, the rejection of the proposal would make our society more iniquitous, less participatory and less democratic. Hence, there is a desperate need to push the government to pass the bill in the Parliament.

At the same time, one cannot totally negate the possibility of unintended outcomes pointed out by the skeptics. In Indian society caste is a dominant form of social relations. Consequently, gender is not only constructed and mediated through caste, but also the nature of gender relations across and between is to a large degree determined by the caste hierarchy. This is quite evident from the experience of the *dalit* women in the political sphere. If the participation of women in general is low, that of the *Dalit* women among them is even lower. Therefore, if reservation was to ensure that women of all social strata would have access to this new political space, a special mechanism has to be created to enable this. Otherwise, only women of the dominant social groups may gain membership. This is more so in the case at the State and Lok Sabha level. The logic of solidarity has to be one of downcasting and downclassing, not just social upliftment.

The question is how does one make it possible for women of all strata to become a part of this process. One of the ways is to take cue from the Karnataka PRI experience of interrelating the quota for women with other reserved categories. In Karnataka one-third of seats within each category, such as SC, ST, OBC and general, were reserved for women. Interestingly, this is not a constitutional requirement, but an intuitive recognition of the fact that women are not a homogeneous category (Batliwala 1996: 88-91). However, one cannot just depend on people's intuitiveness. There just might be a need to think in terms of quotas within quotas—OBC within women's quota, women's quota within all others and so on (Menon 1997:40).

Or else the political parties may need to change their political structure. For example, the political parties of the Scandinavian countries and others like Germany and the Netherlands follows the 40 per cent quota system. This ensures the participation of large number of women in the political sphere. In the case of India, the political parties can have a caste-based quota system. This system adopted by each political party will automatically ensure the participation of not only greater number of women in the elections but also the participation of the marginalised women.

The Reservation Bill and Beyond

In other, words, reservation bill, as already pointed out, is the most necessary and enabling step towards women's political participation. While it is true that in spite of all the State guarantees and legislations women's position has not really changed much. However, that does not mean that one only waits for the big revolution to take place and lets the State go scot-free. At least the provision would make it possible for the women to stake their claim to some extent. Therefore, the biggest challenge before Indian democracy and all those crusading for women's empowerment is to keep the bill from getting squashed or diluted in the Parliament. For if the bill gets passed India will be reaching a new height in the field of gender equality and also setting an example for the so-called developed world to follow. However, if the bill fails to see the day of the light, it will be yet another black day in the history of Indian democracy and the women's movement.

However, one cannot just stop with it. There is a need to go beyond the bill and evolve a transformative approach. The bill is aimed at correcting the inequitable outcomes of social arrangements without disturbing the underlying framework that generates it. Whereas the transformatives remedies, in contrast, are remedies aimed at correcting inequitable outcomes precisely by restructuring the underlying generative framework (Fraser 1995).

Given the multiplication of social antagonisms and the growing appeal of the communal politics, the task has become specially pressing. And the first step towards it, is for the women's movement to mobilise and integrate the interests of all women belonging to the different sections of Indian society.

NOTES

Deshpande, S. 1998. 'Current Impasse in language of Rights: Questions of Context', *Economic and Political Weekly,* January 31.

Fraser, Nancy. 1995. From Redistribution of Recognition? Dilemmas of Social Justice in a Post-Socialist Age; *New Left Review.* No. 212, pp. 68-92.

Menon, N. 1997. Reservations and Representation. *Seminar.* September. pp. 38-41.

Maitheryi, K. 1998. *Women and the Public Domain: Critical Issues for Women's Studies.* February 21, pp. 391-396.

Nanivadekar, M. 1998. 'Reservation for Women: Challenges of Tackling Counter Productive Trend's. *Economic and Political Weekly,* July 11-17, pp.1815-1819.

Roy Choudhury, A. 1998. 'Against Patriarchy', *The Pioneer,* 9 September.

Srilata, B. 1996. Empowering Women. *Seminar,* pp 88-91.

Sadananda, J.S. 1998. 'The Dilemmas of Social Justice and the Current Indian Politics, *Social Action,* April-June, pp. 113-123.

Singhavi, A.M. 1997. The Women's Reservation Bill. *Seminar,* September.

11

POLITICS IN PROTECTIVE DISCRIMINATION
A Case of Uttarakhand

K.N. BHATT

The Constitution of India bears special responsibility for protecting the disadvantaged groups of our society to bring about egalitarian and secular social order based on the concepts of liberty and equality. According to Goodin, the principle of protecting the vulnerable amounts to an injunction to prevent harm from befalling people. This is the responsibility of the State which amounts to the protection of the vital interest, self-respect and civil liberties of its people including the disadvantaged. Failure to discharge a responsibility is failure to produce the desired consequences.[1] The process of development initiated in India as an instrument to bring social transformation may have been successful in multiplying 'GNP' and creating a few 'islands' of growth and prosperity, but it has failed to ensure fair and equitable distribution of the fruits of development among various socio-economic groups and regions. Legitimized by claims of popular mandate, ruling elite succeeded in 'institutionalized exploitation[2] of the disadvantaged, marginalised social groups and backward areas. This has led to 'the polarization of social groups into centre and peripheries'[3] Refusal to the justified claims of the peripheral groups by the elite located at the centre is consequently breeding the climate of conflicts, tensions and mass movements in contemporary Indian society.

Our age-old traditions of unity in diversity and social and ethnic co-existence appear to be at stake. Why the principle of 'uniformity' could not succeed in attaining the goal of protecting the disadvantaged to bring about an 'egalitarian social order'? Are the programmes for change relevant for the socio-economic groups and geo-physical regions in context? If the changes are imposed in utter disregard to socio-economic characteristics of an area, what are its consequences and possible corrective initiatives? These are some of the basic questions in the context of the policy of protective discrimination visualized as an instrument of effecting social change and welfare of the socially deprived sections of our society. Taking an example of Uttarakhand region in Uttar Pradesh, which is one of the most backward areas of the State, lacking basic infrastructural facilities with rampant unemployment, resource scarcity and poverty, the relevance of the State policy of reservation for backward castes is analyzed. It studies the operation of the strategy of compensatory discrimination for mitigating inequalities in an area where presence of the beneficiaries of the programme is negligible and which is still in a state of deprivation. And, how dangerous it is to handle affirmative action on reservations in an area without having any regard to its 'given set of circumstances'.

The essay is divided into three sections. The first section deals with the general state of development in Uttarakhand region and the problems of socio-economic inequalities its people suffer. The second part discusses the policy of protective discrimination as practised by the State and its role in inciting frequent social conflicts in the regions that finally led to a mass movement for a separate State of Uttarakhand. An attempt is made in the third part to summarize the basic issues and problems in the context of initiating desired changes in the policy.

I

The enchanting borderland of the central Himalayas in the State of Uttar Pradesh, which has generally remained unknown to the outside world for a long time, came into focus internationally during recent years with the emergence of a mass movement by its people for a separate Uttarakhand State. Forming one out of the five development planning regions of U.P., Uttarakhand presently consists of twelve districts with 4.23 per cent of the State's population and 17.4 per cent of its geographical area.[4] With more than four-fifth of the region's area being mountainous and one-fifth only belonging to the plains part, its people trace their existence in the milieu of shared cultural traditions and historical memories. It extends from the low lands of Tarai, Bhabar and Doon to the snow-fed mighty peaks of upper Himalayas, demarcating the international borderlines of India with China (Tibet) and Nepal. Providing security cover to the nation and standing as 'water tower' of the country, the Himalaya today appears to be stripped of its rich bio-diversity and the so termed 'inexhaustible' natural resources even after fifty years of development efforts in independent India. The standards of living and day-to-day life of the people in the mountainous parts of both Kumaon and Garhwal divisions of the region have stood still and even deteriorated in some parts, since the days of colonial rule, barring a narrow strip of the land in plains part including Tarai and Doon. In the government records, however, a rosy picture of development is painted by combining this small proportion of area for the region as a whole.

The rich and diversified agrarian economy of this isolated hill region experienced merciless exploitation of its natural resources during the colonial rule which were once described by the British administrators as boundless and 'inexhaustible'.[5] The process of exploitation not only led to the sign of decay and depletion of the inexhaustible resources, but also brought imbalances in native production systems related to agriculture, animal husbandry, forestry and allied self-sustaining economic activities. After Independence the area continued to be exploited with an accelerated pace to fulfil the demands of development projects elsewhere in the country. It remained neglected and isolated from the mainstream of the national life till 1962, particularly because of our wrong notion that the Himalayas are inaccessible and have comparatively lesser contribution in the Net National Product of our economy. The China war of 1962 from our Northern Borders, however, exposed the deficiencies inherent in the strategic area and threw up the challenge of developing and integrating the region into the national mainstream from alienation and separation. The priority of the defence needs in the development planning agenda of the regions gave the planning process a slightly different orientation. Thus, whereas elsewhere in the State and country the principal aim of the first four plans was to build efficient physical and institutional infrastructure for social and economic development, the focus of development effort in the region for a long time continued to remain geared to the fulfilment of defence needs like building of border roads, defence outstations, telecommunication network, etc. to improve the efficiency of the military force inside the area right upto the McMahon Line in the middle sector of the country.[6]

No similar attempt was made to harness the 'comparative advantage' of the region's resources in initiating horticulture, agro-forestry based small scale household industries, location of pollution-free electronic and precision instrument industries, tapping abundant hydro-electric power through environment friendly micro and mini hydel projects, utilizing the skills of educated youth, trained ex-army personnel, hardworking and energetic women power, etc., while formulating social and economic development schemes for a holistic and sustainable development of the region. Because of this ad-hocism and attachment to sectoral myopic vision in formulating and planning of development schemes, the regional economy today is facing the problems of acute resource scarcity, poverty and unemployment.

The agriculture continues to be the mainstay of nearly 75 per cent of total working population of the region and main source of livelihood of over 90 per cent rural households. Due to uneven nature of terrain, cultivable land is scarce and land holdings scattered and fragmented. The pressure on land is excessive as there are 17.6 persons per hectare of cultivable land against 2.3 to 5.8 persons per hectare for rest of the State.[7] The most glaring deficiency of agriculture lies in respect of utilization of its natural advantage in irrigation. With nearly 5 per cent of the region's surface area covered with perennial rivers and streams barely 10 to 12 per cent of the gross cropped area was irrigated in the mountainous parts of the region during 1991-92. In the absence of alternative source of livelihood, people are forced to carry on the non-market oriented and subsistence agricultural activities with old and traditional methods of cultivation. As a result, for most of the cultivating households agricultural produce is barely sufficient to meet their food requirements of 3 to 4 months in a year[8] and less than one per cent of the households could afford to sell their produce in the market.[9] The main source of income for the majority of the households constitutes the money orders sent by the migrant male members employed outside the region in far-off places. A study of some villages in Bhikiasain Block in Almora district of U.P. Hills found that 60 per cent of the family income is earned by migrant males and sent through money orders to their homes which mostly is used as consumption expenditure.[10]

The forests are among the most spectacular of all the natural resources of the hill economy. They preserve not only the eco-stability of the region, but also transfer vital energy to agriculture and animal husbandry sectors for their survival. Due to the excessive exploitation after the advent of colonial rule as well as after Independence forests in the area today stand very badly damaged. Though in the government records nearly two-third of the region's area is reported to be under forest cover, recent satellite survey based data shows only 4.4 per cent of the area has forests with a crown density of 6.0 per cent,[11] scattered over a few pockets of the region. As a consequence, the area is facing recurring problems of soil erosion, landslides, unexpected floods in mountain rivers, drying up of natural water holes/springs, sinking of glaciers—the main sources of water for almost all the major rivers of North India, silting or river beds and dams, etc. For a head-load of fuel wood or leafy fodder, women and children are forced to travel 15 to 20 km distance a day. Similarly, the acute scarcity of water in the hill villages could be noticed even by a casual visitor to the region during summer months when people walk miles away to fetch a bucket of potable water due to drying up of the natural springs around their villages.

The positive impacts of the efforts to diversify regional economy by creating an industrial sector after Independence also remained invisible in terms of generating employment and income for the people, particularly in the mountainous part of the area. Its negative impacts in damaging the fragile eco-systems of the hills, however, could be easily assessed by observing the digging, and blasting operations of the industrial establishments dealing with the extraction of underground mineral resources, particularly magnesite, calcium, phosphate, talcum stones, etc. The industrial development in the area, unfortunately, was initiated without properly identifying the 'comparative advantage' of agro-forestry based production units, small hydro-electricity projects, cool and dust-free environment for the location of electronics and precision tools industries, handicrafts production of herbals and other such medicines, agricultural instruments, etc. by induction of appropriate environment friendly technology which could have generated enough employment and income for the local people and helped in protecting the environment.

The geo-physical features, climate, socio-economic and cultural realities and the peculiar problems of development in the region make it entirely distinct from the plains part of the State. The region today is facing twin problems of 'shortage' of basic infrastructural and community facilities for its sparse and scattered population on the one hand, and 'high cost' of developing and maintaining these facilities on the other. Due to the paucity of resources, skilled employees from the plains parts avoid their postings in the hills which at times, poses severe problems for the proper implementation of development projects in the area. To deal with these problems no serious efforts were made by the government to evolve programmes for strengthening human resource development and management organizations at the local level.

II

After analyzing the special features of the hill economy and its problems of social and economic backwardness, this section is devoted to a discussion on policy of the State government to impose 27 per cent reservation for backward classes in admission to existing educational institutions in Uttarakhand which historically has only about 2 per cent of its population belonging to these caste categories. It also analyzes how the reservation policy imposed in the region in the name of 'uniformity' within the State precipitated spontaneously the demand for a separate State that may have surfaced in the area among a handful of isolated individuals or academic discussions since thirties, but the idea never got popular imagination to turn it into a mass movement of such magnitude which is being witnessed during the past three to four years. And how the instrument of protective discrimination for bringing social equity was turned into practice to mislead the people and play with their sentiments.

With the imposition of 27 per cent reservation for OBCs in educational opportunities in the public sector jobs by the government of Uttar Pradesh in July, 1994, the people of Uttarakhand immediately came out in the streets in protest against the order. In the beginning it was completely a non-political movement, which spontaneously got complete support of the common people in the region. They focussed their agitation by making demand for the formation of a separate State instead of protesting against the immediate cause of reservation for OBCs. The movement immediately got mass support primarily because of the refusal by the government to recognize the distinct features of the region and the problems of backwardness it suffers from. It was also feared that in the event of transmigration of OBCs belonging to other parts of the State for admission in educational institutions in the region, local people would be deprived of their primary means of survival that is finding a job in the employment market of the country through acquisition of educational qualifications. The people, therefore, believed that the only option left with them was to agitate for the formation of Uttarakhand which means getting rid of the impending dangers for their only means of survival.

In fact, the people of the region started their agitation as they have substantial basis for it. There existed unanimous resolutions passed in the two houses of U.P. Legislature twice at different points of time for the formation of a separate State, first in 1991 and second in 1994 respectively. These resolutions were passed with due considerations to the region's distinct typographical, social, economic and administrative compulsions and forwarded to the central government to formalize the grant of State autonomy to the area. Prior to the approval of second resolution, the State government sought to be guided by a high level cabinet committee on Uttarakhand which is also known as the Kaushik Committee, 1994. The Committee after deliberating on various issues related to the socio-economic and geophysical features of the region and the subject on why the hill areas of the State need to be identified as a separate province, submitted its report in two volumes. It scanned all evidences and historical material on the subject and drew a conclusion that the problems in Uttarakhand region are entirely different in comparison to the plain areas of the State and the region needs to be carved out as a separate State. On being fully convinced by the report of the Committee, the members of both the houses of the legislature while passed unanimous resolutions for granting autonomy as a State to Uttarakhand, on the one hand the State, on the other, ruthlessly suppressed the genuine aspirations of the people. In the name of maintaining law and order, a large number of peaceful citizens were killed, women were molested and their modesty outraged at Muzaffarnagar on October 2, 1994 when proceeding to Delhi to negotiate for granting autonomy of a province with the central government.

Earlier in the month of September 1994, the Khatima and Mussoorie firing by the State police left about twenty people dead and two hundred injured in addition to several such ugly incidents in the ongoing agitation for Uttarakhand throughout the region. Rest of the events that unfolded after these incidents and the role played by the State is a part of the history and known to everyone. Within the scope of this essay, only a few lines of the historic judgment of a Bench of the Hon'ble High Court of Allahabad would be sufficient to understand as to what role the State has played in violating the human rights of the citizens, belonging to the area. The court delivered its judgment on February 6, 1996 and concluded that:

> "Thus as the record stands, the High Court holds the State administration of Uttar Pradesh, at the relevant time, responsible for the constitutional torts. Human rights were violated by the let and demur, deliberate or otherwise, and abject silence was shown by the administration on whatever was suffered by the civil rights activists from the hills in furthering a cause which State politics as a formality had committed to them. Death by shooting, concealing

the bodies of the dead, rape of women, molestation of them, and detention of women and children indeed against the provisions of the Constitution of India and substantive and procedural law of the land debased the Rule of Law. No official agency of the State of Uttar Pradesh accepts the reality of the tragedies. The effort throughout the proceedings was to filibuster the proceedings on any pretext which could achieve the result. The means adopted to shake the court from inquiring, within and out, would if it succeeds render the judicature system ineffective".[12]

The Hon'ble High Court in another judgment related to 27 per cent reservation for OBCs in the area posed a very relevant question that whether a geographical area in its accepted economic backwardness and socio-ethnic diversity could be exempted from accommodating alien backwardness? In an answer to this question, the court opined that:

"Reservation under the Constitution of India is nothing but abstraction of mitigating inequalities which in the reality of the social fabric is writ large with lack of balance, socially and economically. Thus, whether reservation under the Constitution is understood as a concept of mitigating inequalities, competing equalities or compensatory discrimination, as a theory put into practice it does not and cannot operate in a vacuum. Its playground is a given set of circumstances, of people and in an area writ large with societal inequalities. In the absence of these factors it is dangerous to handle affirmative action on reservation as it breeds cancer like hate in a conflicting community" (High Court, Allahabad, 1996, pp. 53-54).[13]

The policy, therefore, has to operate as a true instrument of social justice. The beneficiaries may belong to any caste, community, geographical unit or within these categories. Disputes arising out of the policy of reservation in the context of geographical criteria came to be challenged in different High Courts and Supreme Court of India from time to time. The Courts in most of the cases permitted to continue with the criteria keeping in view the socio-economic parameters of the region under reference. In this context, the decision of the Supreme Court delivered in November 1974, in a case (State of U.P. *Vs* Pradeep Tandon), summarizes the status of Uttarakhand regions and its people as under:

"Backwardness is judged by economic basis that each region has its own measurable possibilities for maintenance of human numbers, standards of living and fixed property. From an economic point of view classes of citizens are backward when they do not make effective use of resources. When large areas of land maintain a sparse, disorderly and illiterate population whose property is small and negligible the element of social backwardness is observed. When effective territorial specialization is not possible in the absence of means of communication and technical process as in the hills and Uttarakhand areas the people are socially backward classes of citizens. Neglected opportunities and people in remote places raise walls of social backwardness of people... Educational backwardness is ascertained with reference to these factors. Where people have traditional apathy for education on account of social environmental condition or occupational handicap, it is an illustration of educational backwardness. The hill and Uttarakhand areas are inaccessible. There is lack of educational institutions and education aids. People in the hill and Uttarakhand areas illustrate the educationally backward classes of citizens because lack of educational facilities keep them stagnant and they have neither meaning and values nor awareness for education."[14]

In spite of the clear understanding of the problems of these hills at intellectual and planning level as well as the directions provided by the highest courts of the land, the practicality of the vote politics has prevailed to play with the future and well-being of the simple and hardworking people of the region. The difference in theory and practice and the lack of commitment on the part of the ruling elite resulted in wide-spread violence and social conflicts in the area which virtually have put these 'mountains on fire'.

III

Thus, the theory of protective discrimination is nothing but an instrument of helping those who have remained disadvantaged, marginalised or deprived of opportunities. The Constitution of India makes provisions, as an 'exception' to the guarantee of equality to its citizens, for mitigating inequalities from among these socially and economically deprived sections of our society. As noted earlier, the State government of Uttar Pradesh had fully accepted and acknowledged in its official policy statements that the Himalayan region of the State is very backward and diverse in all respects from other parts of the plain areas and its diversity needs to make it a separate State. This was confirmed through two unanimous resolutions of the State legislature prior to the imposition of 27 per cent reservation for OBCs who are in fact not available but negligibly represented in the region. In these circumstances the State government perhaps wanted to transmigrate the population from other developed regions to fill the vacancies in the hills, depriving the citizens of the area from their justified claims who themselves are very backward. The peculiar situation in the same context is finely summarized by putting an interrogative mark in its judgment by the High Court of Allahabad (1995: 27) as under: "How will the exceptions to the guarantee of equality under the Constitution apply, when in diversity, the exceptions do not exist?"[15]

Thus, these circumstances make it crystal clear how the theory of protective discrimination was used by the practitioners of our democratic polity. It is only this politics in application of the principle of uniformity within the State that has precipitated the current agitation in Uttarakhand for the formation of a separate State. Commenting on the situation, professor C.H. Hanumantha Rao[16] writes:

> "superficially speaking, this agitation for separate statehood would appear to be a means to get over the reservations issue. But fundamentally, this represents a protest against the refusal to recognize the special features of the hill region and the disabilities it suffers from. It is a protest against the prevailing practice of administering the hill regions through remote control by applying 'uniform' yardsticks throughout the State despite the great regional diversity in this large State. The Hill areas of Uttar Pradesh continued to remain backward with meagre opportunities for livelihood on account of defective development strategy and ineffective implementation schemes. This is a consequence of a 'strait jacket' approach inherent in a large State. But for these reasons, the agitation for the formation of Uttarakhand would not have assumed such serious propositions. Therefore, this agitation in neither accidental nor unexpected. Indeed, if there was no objective basis for separate statehood, the agitation would have been focused on the percentage of reservation in jobs as such."

The contradictions within the politics of the State government, therefore assumed such serious magnitude of social conflicts in the area and a crisis at national level. These practices of protective discrimination have not only generated social tensions in Uttarakhand region, but also created similar circumstances in several backward regions of other States also. The problems in these backward regions were created by sacrificing their interests for the benefit of developed regions, mostly due to the compulsions of real politics or vote politics in the prevailing democratic set-up of our political economy. In spite of a number of existing institutional provisions, institutional mechanism and clearly guiding principles of expert opinions for safeguarding the interests of the backward areas, this continued to happen. The examples of such neglect can be clearly found in the regions like Jharkhand, Vidarbha, Marathwada, Rayalseema, Telengana, Saurashtra and Kutch belonging to the different States of Indian union.

To conclude, the concept of protective discrimination while used as an instrument of social transformation to bring about an egalitarian social order could be of great help in the service of humanity. However, its use as a tool to perpetuate institutionalized exploitation of the disadvantaged by the practitioners of real politics breeds social conflicts and tensions in a society, as noted for example in the case of Uttarakhand. The role of the State in bringing social justice towards empowering the common people by providing them freedom of choice, widening economic opportunities and improving their skills and capabilities need not be overemphasized. All this requires clarity of objectives and commitment on the part of the State and its polity, to ensure social justice to its citizens.

The failure of the State governments particularly in case of large States, to provide adequate infrastructural facilities in backward regions in general and community and social services for the weaker sections, is leading to regional disparities and inequalities of income in several parts of the country. It is, therefore, essential for the States to influence such balance, to quote Rao,[17] 'in a direction that is human and equitable' by putting an order of 'good governance' on the top of their agenda for reforms. Implementation of the policy of protective discrimination in the real spirit of the word would effect the desired changes in the process of social transformation, not the playing of politics out of it.

REFERENCES

1. Goddin, R.E. *Protecting the Vulnerable: A Reanalysis of Our Social Responsibilities,* University of Chicago Press, London, 1985.

2. Lal, A.K. 'Politics of Protection: A Case Study of Bihar', in Vimal P. Shah and B.C. Agrawal (eds.), *Reservation: Policy Programmes and Issues*, Rawat Publications, Jaipur, pp. 120-130,1986.
3. Kananaikil, Jose (1986), Equal Rights, Unequal Opportunities and the Future Democracy,' in Vimal P. Shah and B.C. Agrawal (eds.), *Reservation: Policy, Programmes and Issues*, Rawat Publications, Jaipur, pp.13-31,
4. Census of India (1991), Uttar Pradesh, Provisional Population Totals, Series-25, Paper I.
5. Guha, Ramchandra (1989), *The Unquiet Woods: Ecological Change and Peasant Resistance in Himalaya*, Oxford University Press, New Delhi.
6. Bhatt, K.N. (1997), *Uttarakhand: Ecology, Economy and Society*, Horizon Publishers Allahabad.
7. Moddie, A.D., 'Himalayan Environment', J.S. Lall and A.D. Moddie., (eds). *The Himalaya: Aspects of Change*, India International Centre, Oxford University Press, Delhi, 1981.
8. Bhatt, K.N. (1997), *Uttarakhand: Ecology, Economy and Society*, Horizon Publishers, Allahabad.
9. Joshi. B.K., Agricultural Economy of Uttarakhand: Preliminary Results of a Study Based on A Survey of Eight Village Clusters, In SHERPA, Seminar Papers on Rainfed Agriculture in the Himalayan Regions of India, 10-12 Jan., 10 Pant Nagar, 1987.
10. Planning Commission, Report of the Task Force for the Study of Eco-Development in Himalayan Regions, Government of India, New Delhi, 1982.
11. Singh S.P., and J.S. Singh, 'Structure and Functions of Forest Ecosystems of Central Himalaya', in J.S. Singh (eds.). *Environmental Regeneration in Himalaya*. CHEA & Gyanodaya Prakashan, Nainital, pp. 85-113. 1985.
12. High Court of Judicature at Allahabad (1996), *Uttarakhand Sangharsh Samiti* Vs *State of Uttar Pradesh*, Judgment Delivered on February 9, Allahabad.
13. High Court of Judicature at Allahabad (1995), *Manvendra Shah* Vs *State of Uttar Prad*esh, Judgment Delivered on May 31, Allahabad.
14. Supreme Court of India, *Pradeep Tandon* Vs *State of Uttar Pradesh*, Judgment Reported in AIR, 1975 SC 563, Quoted in The High Court of Judicature at Allahabad (1995), *Manvendra Shah* Vs *State of Uttar Pradesh*, Judgment Delivered on May 31, Allahabad, pp. 20-21, 1975.
15. High Court of Judicature at Allahabad (1995), *Manvendra Shah* Vs *State of Uttar Pradesh*, Judgment Delivered on May 31, Allahabad.
16. Rao, C.H. Hanumantha, 'Uttarakhand: Case for a Separate State,' *Mainstream*, Annual Number, December 20,19, pp. 25-28, 1997.
17. Rao, C.H. Hanumantha, 'Uttarakhand: Case for a Separate State,' *Mainstream*, Annual Number, December 20,19, pp. 25-28, 1997.

12

PROTECTIVE DISCRIMINATION AND THE SCHEDULED CASTES
Views of Dr. B. R. Ambedkar

SHAILENDRA KUMAR TIWARY

B. R. Ambedkar was born in the Mahar community of Maharashtra and had himself suffered from such injustices from which members of the scheduled castes had suffered in India. Naturally, therefore, it became the first mission of his life to fight against these injustices and to secure to the members of the scheduled castes their due place in the Hindu social order. It was for this purpose that he supported positive discrimination for them.

Protective discrimination, it may be pointed out, is a kind of discrimination in favour of members of a certain group in order to rectify inequality of opportunity that is inherent in the social structure. Its purpose is to permit discrimination in favour of such groups for a period, which have suffered from such structural injustices with a view to overcome such injustices.

In order to understand the view of Dr. Ambedkar on protective discrimination it is necessary to keep in mind three things, viz. his view of an ideal social order, his view of the Hindu social order based on the system of four *varnas*, and finally, his view of protective discrimination in order to remove the structural injustices from the Hindu social order. I have divided this chapter in three parts. In the first part I have discussed his concept of an ideal social order as well as Ambedkar's view on the existing form of the Hindu social order: in the second part I have discussed his view of protective discrimination; in the third part I have tried to derive certain conclusions.

I

According to Dr. Ambedkar an ideal social order should be based on two foundations, namely, justice and utility. Justice implies equality. If all men are equal, all men are of the same essence and the common essence entitled to them to have the same fundamental rights and to equal liberty. He believed that justice is another name for liberty, equality and fraternity. Liberty, in order to be real, must be accompanied by certain social conditions. In the first place, there should be social equality, in the second place there should be economic security and in the third place there should be proper condition to make knowledge available to all. Fraternity, he thought, is opposed to individualism and implies fellow-feeling. It lies in the sentiment which leads an individual to identify himself with the good of others where fraternity prevails, an individual does not think rest of his fellow creatures as struggling rivals. According to Dr. Ambedkar individualism would produce anarchy. It is only fraternity which prevents it and helps to sustain the moral order among men.[1]

These three principles of liberty, equality and fraternity are not to be treated as separate items. They form what he called 'a union of trinity'. To divorce one from the other, he stated in his last lecture in the Constituent Assembly, is to defeat the very purpose of a democratic social order.[2]

The other foundation of an ideal social order, he thought, is its utility to all its members. There is in fact no antagonism between justice and utility: what is unjust to the individual, he said, cannot be useful to the society.[3]

It was in reference to this notion of an ideal social order that Dr. Ambedkar analysed the Hindu social order based on the theory of four *varnas*.

In his paper entitled 'Castes in India' that he presented in a seminar held at the Columbia University in 1916 he observed that at the outset the Hindu society was composed of four classes which were the Brahmins or the priestly class, the Kshatriyas or the military class, the Vaishyas or the merchant class, and the Shudras or the artisan or the menial class. This was essentially a class system in which individuals, when qualified, could change personnel. He further observed:

> "This sub-division of a society is quite natural. But un-natural thing about these sub-divisions is that they have lost the open door character of the class system and have become self-enclosed units called castes."[4]

The development of the caste system had adverse effect on the Hindu society. Its effect on the Hindus was deplorable. It not only killed public spirit but also destroyed the sense of public charity and made the formation of public opinions impossible. The Hinduism social order lost its sense of justice and came to be based on what he called 'graded inequality'.[5] There was debasement of human personality. Hinduism based on the caste system lost not only social equality but also economic security as it denied to its members freedom of vocation. It also restricted the spread of knowledge. The utility of such a social system was no longer the same for all its members. He stated in his '*Annihilation of Caste*':

> "Castes does not result in economic efficiency. Caste cannot and has not improved the race. Caste has however done one thing. It has completely disorganised and demoralized the Hindus".[6]

The worst sufferer was the menial class known as the *shudras*. They became untouchables which was, according to Ambedkar, an indirect form of slavery. Comparing the two, he pointed out that slavery was never obligatory but untouchability was. Once an individual was born as an untouchable he was subject to all disabilities of an untouchable. The Hindu social order became a worst type of an unfree social order.[7]

Ambedkar believed that unless the principles of equality and fraternity were established in the social order, India cannot be a nation in a true sense of the word. Every effort must therefore be made to make India 'the Indian nation'.[8] It was to secure this end that he fought throughout his life and pleaded for protective discrimination in order to rectify the structural injustices done to the scheduled castes.

II

In his advocacy of protective discrimination for scheduled castes, Ambedkar laid particular emphasis on three aspects, namely, special provision for their proper education, provisions to end any kind of social discrimination and provisions to ensure their due representation in the legislature, the executive and the public services.

Dr. Ambedkar realised at an early stage that without proper education it was not possible to ensure development of the depressed classes. He submitted a lengthy statement concerning the state of education of the depressed classes in Bombay presidency on behalf of the Bahishkrita

Hitakarini Sabha to the Indian Statutory Commission (1928) in which he emphasised the need of sincerity on the part of the government in the matter of promoting their education.[9] Again in 1942 in his memorandum submitted to the Governor-General outlining the grievances of the scheduled castes, he emphasised the importance of their educational grievances specially in the sphere of science and engineering as well as advanced education in foreign universities.[10] In 'States and Minorities' (1947) he recommended provisions concerning their education as one of the special responsibilities of the United States of India and suggested that the Union and the States should assume financial responsibility for their primary, secondary and higher education. It should be the responsibility of the Union Government for finding money for their foreign education and there should be separate budgetary allocation for this purpose.[11]

He was equally concerned for putting an end to any kind of social discrimination that prevailed in the Hindu Society. In his memorandum that he, together with R. Srinivasan, submitted to the Minority sub-committee of the Round Table Conference (1930-31) he laid down certain terms and conditions on which the depressed classes would consent to place themselves under a majority rule in a self-governing India. These included the demand for equal citizenship and free enjoyment of equal rights.[12]

In 'States and Minorities' (1947) Ambedkar again recommended a list of fundamental rights of citizens which included provisions to end social discrimination. For example, clause 1 recommended abolition of any privilege or disability arising out of rank, birth, persons, famiiy, religion or religious usage and custom. In clause 3, it was stated that citizens 'are equal before the law and possess equal civic rights'. He wanted that these rights should be justiciable and the Supreme Court should have the power to issue appropriate prerogative writs on the application of an aggrieved party. Later most of these rights were included as fundamental rights embodied in Part III of the Indian Constitution.[13]

In this respect he particularly referred to conditions prevailing in Indian villages where the caste Hindus could use the weapon of social boycott against the depressed classes. As depressed classes had no economic independence in villages it was used not only as a social but also as economic boycott.[14]

Social boycott, he said, was always held over the heads of the untouchables by the caste Hindus as a 'Sword of Damocles'.[15] From this point of view he was critical of so-called village republic where there was no room for social equality. He wrote, 'If it is a republic, it is the republic of touchables by the touchables and for the touchables.'[16] He was sole member of the Constituent Assembly to criticise villages as "a sink of localism, a den of ignorance, narrow mindedness and communalism".[17] He therefore wanted that social boycott should be declared a cognizable offence.[18] He also wanted that the Constitution should provide for new settlements for the scheduled castes in separate villages. There should be a settlement commission under the new Constitution to hold uncultivated lands belonging to the States in trust for the settlement of the Scheduled Castes.[19] Obviously, these ideas have inspired the schemes for the establishment of the so-called 'Ambedkar Villages' in many parts of the country.

Finally, Dr. Ambedkar favoured reservation for scheduled castes in the legislature, the executive and the public services. He believed that unless the depressed classes had a share in political power, they would not get their just place in the social order. It was from this point of view that he demanded a *Swaraj* constitution in the plenary session of the First Round Table Conference, held in London in 1930. He said.

> "It is only in Swaraj constitution that we stand any chance of getting the political power into our hand without which we cannot bring salvation to our people."[20]

Ambedkar believed that the problem of the scheduled castes was not merely social, but also political and, therefore, participation in the sharing of political power was an effective means to solve their problems. He said:

> "We are often remained that the problem of the depressed classes is a social problem and that its solution lies elsewhere than in politics. We take strong exception to this view. We hold that the problem of the depressed classes will never be solved unless they get political power in their own hands."[21]

He, therefore, favoured reservation of seats for the scheduled castes according to their population. In his memorandum to the Governor-General on grievances of the scheduled castes (1942) he observed that they had inadequate representation in the Central Legislature, Central Executive and in Public Services. As the population of the scheduled castes was very near to that of the Muslims, they should have the same ratio of representations.[22]

In the matter of reservations he claimed a parity with other minority groups. According to Ambedkar basis of a minority should not only be religion but also social discrimination. The scheduled castes should, therefore, be accepted as a minority. They had suffered like other minority groups. In fact they had suffered from worst kind of civil disabilities and should, therefore, have additional safeguard, to enable them to improve their condition in the social order.[23] He was opposed to any constitutional scheme for independent India in which the scheduled castes were treated on a lower plane than other minority groups. This was precisely the ground on which he criticised the Cripps Proposal (1942) and the Cabinet Plan of May 16, 1946.[24]

However with the partition of the country there came momentous changes in the political and constitutional scenario of the country. The Constituent Assembly which had begun its functioning under the Cabinet Mission Plan of May 16, 1946, was influenced by these developments. In the changed situation it decided to recognise only cultural rights of minorities. But the case of scheduled castes and scheduled tribes were treated separately on the ground of their backwardness. Dr. Ambedkar, the Chairman of the Drafting Committee, defended such changes in the Constituent Assembly.

Most of the principles regarding protective discrimination for scheduled castes as advocated by Dr. Ambedkar were embodied in the Constitution. Art. 15, provided against social discrimination and Art. 17, provided for abolition of untouchability and its practice in any form was forbidden. It was also accepted that there was a need for special effort for educational development of the scheduled castes. Art. 46 provided the State should promote with special care the educational and economic interests of scheduled castes and scheduled tribes and should protect them from social injustice and all forms of exploitation. Art. 340 provided for the appointment of a commission to investigate the conditions of socially and educationally backward classes. The Drafting Committee had provided in the Draft Constitution for reservation of seats for minorities in the House of the People (Art. 292) and in the State legislatures (Art. 294). But in accordance with the decision taken by Advisory Committee on May 11, 1949, which was accepted by the Constituent Assembly, Dr. Ambedkar moved amended articles 292 and 294 of the Draft Constitution in the Constituent Assembly on August 23 and 24, 1949, which provided reservations in the House of the People and the State legislatures only for the scheduled castes and the scheduled tribes respectively.[25] These were accepted by the Assembly and were embodied in the Constitution as Art. 331 and Art. 332 respectively.

He also moved in the Assembly new Article 295A which provided that reservation of seats in the legislatures for scheduled castes and scheduled tribes would cease to exist after ten years.[26] Some members in the Constituent Assembly wanted reservations for longer periods. In his reply to the debate Dr. Ambedkar said:

> "If at the end of ten years the scheduled castes find that their position has not improved or that they want further extension of this period, it will not be beyond their capacity or their intelligence to invent new ways of getting the same protection what they are promised here".[27]

It clearly shows that he was in favour of periodic review of reservations.

The principle of reservation in public services was also accepted. It was provided that the claims of the members of the scheduled castes and scheduled tribes should be considered consistently with the efficiency of administration in the making of appointments to public services.[28]

It was also provided that there should be a special officer for the scheduled castes and scheduled tribes to investigate all matters relating to the safeguards provided for them and he should report to the President upon the working of these safeguards.[29]

III

We can say in conclusion that protective discrimination was favoured by Dr. Ambedkar to rectify structural injustices done to certain groups in society especially the scheduled castes. He intended to establish a social order based on justice and utility, in which all groups, privileged and unprivileged, should merge into one, there should be no distinction between touchables untouchables or minorities and majorities. All should contribute to the making of the Indian nation in a spirit of fraternity and on the basis of equality. While moving the Draft Constitution for the consideration of the Constituent Assembly, he observed:

> "In this country both the minorities and the majorities have followed a wrong path. It is wrong for the majority to deny the existence of minorities. It is equally wrong for the minorities to perpetuate themselves. A solution must be found which will serve a double

purpose. It must recognize the existence of minorities to start with. It must be also such that it will enable majorities and minorities to merge some day into one".[30]

This equally applies to his attitude towards scheduled castes. And this was, it may be suggested, the real purpose of the principle of protective discrimination as he conceived it.

REFERENCES

1. Dr. Baba Saheb Ambedkar, *Writings and Speeches,* Vol. III, Philosophy of Hinduism, pp. 244.
2. *C.A.D.,* Vol. XI, pp. 979.
3. *Writings and Speeches,* Vol. III, pp. 66-67.
4. *Writings and Speeches,* Vol. I, pp. 17-18.
5. *Writings and Speeches,* Vol. I, Annihilation of Caste, pp. 56.
6. *Writings and Speeches,* Vol. I, *ibid,* p. 50.
7. *Writings and Speeches,* Vol. V, Slaves and Untouchables, pp. 15-18.
8. *C.A.D.* Vol. XI, pp. 981.
9. *Writings and Speeches,*, Vol. III, pp. 407-28.
10. *Writings and Speeches,* Vol. X, pp. 426.
11. *Writings and Speeches,* Vol. I, pp. 402-3.
12. *Writings and Speeches,* Vol. III, pp. 546-50.
13. *Writings and Speeches,* Vol. I, pp. 392-95.
14. *Writings and Speeches,* Vol. III, pp. 547-50.
15. *Writings and Speeches,* Vol. I, p. 416.
16. *Writings and Speeches,* Vol. V, p. 26.
17. C.A.D., Vol. VII, p. 39
18. *Writings and Speeches,* Vol. III, pp. 548-50.
19. *Writings and Speeches,* Vol. I, p. 403.
20. *Writings and Speeches,* Vol. III, p. 505.
21. *Writings and Speeches,* Vol. III, p. 506.
22. *Writings and Speeches,* Vol. X, pp. 410-11.
23. *Writings and Speeches,* Vol. III, pp. 507-8.
24. See his statement on Cripps Proposal (*Writings and Speeches,* Vol. X, p. 455).
25. *C.A.D.,* Vol. IX, pp. 633 and 663.
26. *C.A.D.,* Vol. IX, p. 674.
27. *Ibid,* pp. 696-98.
28. Art. 335.
29. Art. 338. By the Constitution 65th Amendment Act a National Commission was constituted for the purpose.
30. *C.A.D.,* Vol. VII, p. 39.

13

PROTECTIVE DISCRIMINATION
A Quest for Social Justice

JITENDRA NARAYAN

The preamble of the Indian Constitution promises its citizens to award of what is due to them in terms of social justice besides economic and political justice. It would not be out of place to point out that our society had been victim to social discrimination and situation of deprivation, humiliation and exploitation for a section of society, specially Scheduled Castes (SC) and Scheduled Tribes (ST), has remained a special feature of our social and political system. So, in this situation our Constitution really bears a special responsibility for protecting the disadvantaged groups of our society to bring about egalitarian and just social order based on the concept of liberty and equality. The proceedings of the Indian Constituent Assembly were testimony of the fact that the framers of our Constitution were very much conscious of this responsibility. The President of the Constituent Assembly Dr. Rajendra Prasad declared, "To all we give the assurance that it will be our endeavour to end poverty and squalor, and its companions hunger and disease, to abolish distinctions and exploitation and to ensure decent conditions of living...."[1] Other national leaders of the higher echelon also expressed similar desires. Shri Jawaharlal Nehru, for instance, said, "....The service of India meant ....the service of the millions who suffer.... we have to build up the noble mansion of free India where all her children may dwell...."[2].

In order to meet the abovesaid goal the part XVI of the Constitution deals with special provisions. These are constitutional and legal interventions for socio-economic justice. They seek to change the perception of citizens about themselves and other social groups or *vice-*

versa; change the attitudes and behaviour patterns for individuals and groups and also change their material condition.

The part XVI of the Constitution has special significance to the SC and ST which have been traditionally oppressed and are, consequently, under privileged. These provisions are based on the policy of compensatory discrimination and aim at giving preferential treatment to the SC and ST specially with regard to the provisions of reservation of jobs and reservation of seats in legislatures. This policy falls in line with the definition of social justice of Joel Feinberg who says, "The basic principle of comparative justice (Social Justice) is that like cases are to be treated alike and different cases to be treated differently."[3]

So far as the term Scheduled Caste is concerned it does not stand for a particular caste but it is a group of such people from among the untouchables who have been declared as Scheduled Caste by the President of India. However, the castes that fall within this category are *Sudras* of *Varna Vyavastha,* Harijans (though the term was coined by Narsingh Mehta) Gandhiji, depressed, suppressed or *dalits* of Jotiba Phule, Rama Swaṃi Periyar and Ambedkar and Bahujan Samaj of Maiku Ram, Kanshi Ram and Mayawati.[4]

The specific provisions under the Constitution giving certain safeguards to SC and ST and some other weaker sections of society can be grouped into two parts:

1. Abolition of caste and untouchability; and
2. Special provision relating to certain classes.

First part includes Articles 14, 15, 16 and 17, whereas part second includes Articles 46, 330, 331, 332, 333, 334, 335, 338, 340, 341, 342 and 366(24). Article 14: Right to Equality and Article 15: Prohibition of discrimination on grounds of religion, race, caste, sex or place of birth are designed to protect all the people against discrimination, including the minority community by committing the nation to the idea of basic equality of all the citizens.

Article 16: Equality of opportunity in matters of public employment, states that all citizens will be treated equal in matters relating to the employment in the State. Nobody will be victim of discrimination on grounds of religion, race, caste, sex etc. As these articles were not considered adequate, Article 17: Abolition of untouchability, was added in the interest of the untouchables. It declares that "untouchability is abolished, and its practice in any form is forbidden, the enforcement of any disability arising out of untouchability shall be an offence punishable in accordance with law." Later, in 1955, the Untouchability Offence Act was passed. Under this Act, any person accused of this offence can be tried and punished by the Courts.

The Articles 46, 330, 332, 334, 335 and 338 of the Indian Constitution seek to ameliorate the position of the Scheduled Castes. Article 46 aims at promotion of educational and economic interests of Scheduled Castes, Scheduled Tribes and other weaker sections and promises to protect them from social injustice and all forms of exploitation. Articles 330 and 332 are designed to provide special privileges to Scheduled Castes and Scheduled Tribes in terms of political representation in the House of the People, as well as in the Legislative Assemblies of the States. And Article 335 aims at improving their status economically by considering their claims to services and posts. Article 335 reads:

> "The claims of the members of the Scheduled Castes and the Scheduled Tribes shall be taken into consideration, consistently with the maintenance of efficiency of administration, in the making of appointments to services and posts in connection with the affairs of the Union or of a State."

Under Article 338, a special officer is appointed by the President to investigate all matters relating to the safeguards provided for the Scheduled Castes and Scheduled Tribes under the Indian Constitution and to report to the President upon the working of those safeguards at such intervals as the President may direct and the President shall cause all such reports to be laid before each House of the Parliament.

Articles 331 and 333 provide representation of the Anglo-Indian community by nomination by the President and Governor, in case that community is not adequately represented in the Union and States' Lower Houses.

The privileges in the form of reservation and protections to certain classes as mentioned above, perhaps, constitute the term 'Protective Discrimination' in Indian context. And those who are against this 'Protective Discrimination' argue that it is against the principle of equality of opportunity. According to this argument, human beings are to be judged and rewarded on the basis of individual merit and achievement. So an individual has to compete for places open to persons of comparable talent. So individuals are solely responsible for their success or failure.

However, this argument ignores other side of the problem of inequality. Fair competition can take place only among equals. The possession of certain abilities or lack of them are conditioned by home environment, socio-economic status and equality of education, etc. And Indian history reveals that the Depressed Classes (the untouchables) were left in most intolerable position of helplessness which had no parallel in this world.[5] As we know, Indian society has been rigidly compartmentalized since time immemorial. The society is based on hierarchy, each caste occupying a specific position in the social ladder. The caste system has given rise to social inequality and discrimination which resulted in the condemnation of some sections to subhuman life.[6] The definition of a 'slave' given by Plato was appropriately applicable to the untouchable. Plato has defined the slave as one who accepts from another the purposes which control his conduct. Therefore, Ambedkar pointed out that the untouchables were treated as slaves because "(1) they were so socialized as never to complain of their low state; (2) they never dreamed of trying to improve their lot, by forcing the other classes to treat them with the common respect; (3) the idea that they had been born to their lot was so ingrained in their mind that it never occurred to them to think that their fate was anything so irrevocable; and (4) nothing would ever persuade them that men are all made of same clay or that they have the right to insist on better treatment than that meted out to them.[7]

Ambedkar, himself experienced humiliation throughout his life, as a child, in school, in college and in his first job when he joined as Professor at Syndenham College of Commerce, Bombay. His university educated colleagues objected to his drinking water from the common pot; when he joined the Baroda Civil Service, the peons would not handle his files and the clerks kept themselves at a 'safe' distance.[8] He could not get a place to live in Baroda when he was posted there because he was an untouchable. He tried to live in a Parsi hotel without disclosing his caste, but on discovery, he was humiliated and thrown out. He sent a note to the Maharaja who referred him to the Dewan but the Dewan could not do anything. He spent the night without shelter. Tired, hungry, and fagged out, he sat under a tree and burst into a flood of tears.[9] In short, their (untouchables) social, political, religious and educational conditions were most wretched and deplorable. These strata of Hindu society, on account of their low status, from all angles had been subjected to a variety of disabilities under the traditional system. For thousands of years, the untouchables were victims of injustice and were heartlessly exploited and prevented from rising above the social status fixed for them. Any attempt on the part of anyone to behave in a manner not prescribed by the Hindu society, attracted severe punishment of inhuman nature.[10]

The condition of the untouchables even during the British rule presents a dismal picture of decay, degradation and demoralization. Even the social reform movements like the Brahmo Samaj, the Prarthana Samaj, the Arya Samaj and the Satyashodhak Samaj failed to exert any effective influence in the amelioration of the condition of the untouchables. As the struggle for independence gained momentum the zest for social reform began to subside. The goal before these social reform movements was to solve social problems such as dowry, *sati*, widow remarriage, age of consent, etc., but none of these movements sought to solve the vexed problem of untouchability .[11] Ambedkar knew that the Depressed Classes (the untouchables) had no friend. The British Government too had used them only as an excuse for its continued existence. The Hindus claimed them only to deny them or, to appropriate their rights. The Muhammedans refused to recognize their separate existence, because they feared that their privileges might be curtailed by the admission of a rival. Therefore, the untouchables were depressed by the Government, suppressed by the Hindu and disregarded by the Muslim. Thus, the Depressed Classes (the untouchables) were left in a most intolerable position of helplessness which had no parallel in this world.[12]

To overcome centuries of subjugation, to reshape the society on democratic lines and to promote and safeguard the interests of the underprivileged, the policy of 'Protective Discrimination' was adopted which pays due regard to the claims of SC and ST. Abolition of untouchability through the Constitution was a firm and positive step initiated by the founding fathers of our Constitution. Besides, the policy of reservation was adopted by them as a device through which the underprivileged could climb up the social ladder and stake their claim to positions of power and influence like other sections of society. Replying to the debate on the third reading of the Draft Constitution what Ambedkar pointed out in the Constituent Assembly was very much revealing. To him democracy was nothing but the consummation of the three "principles of liberty, equality and fraternity.... (that) form a union of trinity in the sense that to divorce one from the other is to defeat the very purpose of democracy...."[13] He knew fully well the inadequacies of Indian society to serve as the base for a full-fledged democratic edifice. On such inadequacy was the 'principle of graded inequality', which meant 'elevation for some and degradation for others'. So also in the economic field. It is for these reasons that he said:

> . . . On the 26 January 1950, we are going to enter into a life of contradictions: in politics we will have equality and in social and economic life we will have inequality. In politics we will be recognizing the principle of one man one vote and one vote one value. In our social and economic life, we shall by reason of our social and economic structure, continue to deny the principle of one man one value. How long shall we continue to deny equality in our social and economic life? If we continue to deny it for long, we will do so only by putting our political democracy in peril. We must remove this contradiction at the earliest possible moment or else those who suffer from inequality will blow up the structure of political democracy which this Assembly has so laboriously built up...[14]

Therefore, it would not be irrelevant to suggest that the validity of special protection to Depressed Classes could be understood in the context of Indian society. The degree of social, political and economic disability that a group suffers, should constitute the basis for according special protection, was the philosophy behind the constitutional protection to SC and ST in India. The accommodation of the concept of equality along with preferences, known generally as the "Reservation Policy", which has been legally recognized, constitutionally established, administratively enforced, judicially protected and politically articulated, has however, a century old history of protracted battle against the inequalities of a traditional social order based on distinction by birth. This dualistic feature of the Constitution has been the cause of a great deal of controversy. On the one hand, there is the guarantee of equality for all citizens; and , on the other hand, there is provision for the preferential treatment to Scheduled Castes and Scheduled Tribes and now to backward class (BC) and other backward class (OBC). Now comprehensiveness has reached such length that many religious, ethnic, regional and host of small communities are crying to include themselves into some class or other with an eye on the reservation factor.

So the earlier Scheduled Castes/Scheduled Tribes concept of weaker class, as envisaged by the founding fathers of our Constitution, including Ambedkar, has lost its meaningfulness and relevance. By gradually broadbasing and expanding the scope of the weaker section in already caste-ridden society, we are only reinforcing the artificially described 'Sub-Classes' and stoking the fire of sub-nationalism and caste conflict, but obviously not Marxian in the style of classical Marxian 'Class-

Struggle'. If we go on with this preposterous high-mindedness of safeguarding the interest of every tiny caste or class with an eye on the slice of cake of 'reservation' and associated facilities and fringe benefits, the quota system will cross 100 per cent and we have to invent some new mathematical symbol or model which is larger than 100 per cent and what we may call larger then life reality. As such, the concept of weaker section of the society has been so ill-defined by naive labelling of caste and class that we cannot make much of it except making the confusion worse confounded. No doubt, some political mileage can be always obtained out of this ambiguity in the coming elections.[15]

In a highly competitive political system like ours, it is the numerical strength of any group of people which matters more than anything else. Taking advantage of political competition among political parties these so-called backward sections of society have succeeded in making their socio-economic disabilities as an asset by exploiting their numerical strength. Given the scarcity of resources the search for economic security and affluence generates intense competition. Particularly, when the upper castes find job opportunities for themselves blocked by the entry of untouchables and now by backward castes, they resent it bitterly. The relationship between the upper castes and other castes is seen as Zero-sum game in which the gain of one is considered to be the loss of the others.[16]

However, the upper caste people find it very difficult to reconcile themselves to the fact that their children, even if they do better than their backward, scheduled caste and tribe counterparts and show great promise, are discriminated against in the matter of jobs and employment. They express bitterness against reservation of seats in technical and professional education. Similarly, out of turn departmental promotions evoke bitter criticism. Reservation policy of the Janata Dal during the prime ministership of V.P. Singh further added fuel to the fire. As a result of it, caste consciousness has further increased and is on the increase. Srinivas has observed:

> The tendency to continue to think in terms of backward and forward castes is producing new tensions and difficulties which may become more intractable in the near future. Actually many powerful castes have a vested interest in backwardness and they will resist any attempt to remove them from the backward category.[17]

The egalitarian measures taken by the government and reservation of seats for backward classes taking the help of Article 340 of the Constitution which provides scope to investigate and improve the condition of backward classes, tend to deepen the caste antagonism and that too, particularly at the lower rungs of the caste system. While they fail to equip the Scheduled Castes with equal social and political power, they are causing increasing resentment, particularly among the sections known variously in various States as Backward Castes or Other Backward Castes, whose economic and social power is weak and ineffectual as that of Scheduled Castes. The result has been increasing caste confrontation between the two groups of socially weaker and oppressed sections of society or the caste Hindus as a whole and Scheduled Castes, as in Marathwada. Series of incidents like Kilvemani (1973), Belchi (1977), Marathwada (1978) and Pipra (1979) are symptoms of the situation.[18] Such a process tends to isolate scheduled castes still further from the other sections of society.

The foregoing analysis reveals that the philosophy which was responsible for special provisions, under the Indian Constitution for the socio-economic justice of the weaker sections of the society could not achieve its goal as was conceived by the founding fathers of our Constitution. However, this is not to suggest that there has not been any improvement in the condition of SC and ST and weaker sections of the society. A study suggests that most of the people belonging to Scheduled Castes feel that they are occupying important positions in the society and enjoying certain amount of power and prestige which earlier generation did not.[19]

But in spite of the observations made, other facts reveal that the desired goal of social justice had yet to be achieved. The following tables 13.1, 13.2, and 13.3 are self-explanatory.

Table 13.1: Literacy Rate of SC, ST and Rest of Population

(Percentage)

Year	*SC*	*ST*	*Rest of population*	*Gap between Rest of population and* *SC*	*ST*
1961	10.27	8.53	27.86	17.59	19.33
1971	14.67	11.30	33.80	19.13	22.50
1981	21.38	16.35	41.22	19.84	24.87
1991	37.41	29.60	52.21	14.18	22.61

Source: Eighth Five Year Plan, Census of India, 1991, Series 1.

Table 13.2: Percentage of SC Representation in Government and Public Sector Undertakings

(Percentage)

Category	*Government Sector*		*Public Sector Undertaking*	
	1971	1991	1971	1991
Class I	2.58	2.53	0.52	1.29
Class II	4.06	2.35	1.54	2.31
Class III	9.59	4.98		
Class IV	18.37	6.82		

**Source*: Eighth Five Year Plan, Government of India, Planning Commission, New Delhi: 419.

Table 13.3: Incidence of Poverty

(Percentage)

Year	*Total Population*	*Scheduled Castes*	*Scheduled Tribes*
1977-78	51.2	64.6	72.4
1983-84	40.4	53.1	58.4
1987-88	33.4	44.7	52.6

Source: Eighth Five Year Plan.

The above tables 13.1, 13.2 and 13.3 suggest that the SC and ST have not come at par with the rest of the population. Besides, studies further reveal that the pace of development achieved by the people belonging to SC and ST in terms of percentage has gone to a small section of the people belonging to SC and ST. And the condition of the SC and ST as a whole has not improved much. Deliberations of distinguished scholars participating in a National Seminar on "Protective Discrimination" Ideology and Praxis" held at G.B. Pant Social Science Institute, Allahabad in the month of March 1998 also confirmed this hypothesis.

The Mahars in Maharashtra, the Jatavs in U.P., the Madigas and Malas in Andhra Pradesh, the Chowkidar and Zamindar Meenas in Rajasthan, the Chamar, Dusadh, Dhobi and Pasi in Bihar constitute such privileged groups. In fact they are most empowered. The weakest remain untouched from the benefits as it remains stuck up at the top in the intra-community hierarchy. Poor sections among the excluded communities find themselves twice deprived. Thus it tends to be lop-sided in its effect as it has led to development at upper end and stagnation at the bottom.[20]

Prof. Sachchidananda also observed that:

> "The benefits have been cornered by a cluster of certain kin groups. This is on account of certain structural factors. The better situated among the beneficiaries enjoy a disproportionate share of programme benefits. Compensatory programmes provide the basis for personal achievements and enlarge the beneficiaries' capacities to share their own lives."[21]

The framers of our Constitution had perhaps an apprehension of such a situation. So they had provided an opportunity to the succeeding generations in forms of Articles 341 and 342 of the Constitution, which allow them either to include or exclude any section of society from SC and ST categories.

However, the political development of our country presents a different picture. Today it seems very difficult rather impossible to take this issue in the right perspective because this section of society constitutes large number of population. According to 1991 census the proportion of Scheduled Caste population to total in India was 16.48 per cent. Extension of the policy of reservation to Backward Class (BC) and Other Backward Class (OBC) has further complicated this issue. In other words Scheduled Castes, Scheduled Tribes, Backward Classes, Other Backward Classes and others constituting the weaker section of society offer a substantial vote-bank to contending political parties in a democratic India. These parties are embroiled at times more in struggle for power than upliftment of the weaker section. As a result, conflicts, violence and tension is rife.[22]

The foregoing analysis suggests that the constitutional and legal interventions in forms of compensatory discrimination made to achieve the goal of socio-economic justice, have not produced the desired result. And we are standing far away from the goal of social justice even after 50 years of independence. It has rightly been observed that in the recent years since independence the caste consciousness seems to have grown. The pernicious influence of this caste-ideology is not confined to the upper and well-placed castes, it is not restricted to the non-Harijan castes. The economic changes and political upheavals of India have so little affected the economic basis of casteism that the untouchables themselves are affected by caste considerations. Jagjivan Ram in his book *Challenge of Caste in India* writes: "The effect of this system is so pernicious and all pervading that the majority of the population of the country, which is composed of the backward communities, thinks more of aping the customs and manners of the upper castes and less of breaking the shackles. If the untouchables practise untouchability within their own communities to such a surprising extent it can be explained by the fact that it is a sincere but poor imitation of the Brahmins." In reality it reveals the iron grip of the caste ideology on the untouchables, a grip which has extended over hundreds of years and which they are unable to shake off in spite of the atrocities committed against them. This is how the ideology of the ruling sections continues to dominate the oppressed.[23]

The above description of facts and situation reveals that the policy of protective discrimination has tended to impede national integration and widen social distance between communities enjoying it and other sections of society. The political dimension has overshadowed the socio-economic issues involved. However, the remedies for removal of social and economic inequalities lie not alone in political or legal action but in changing the social structure and they also need to look at reservation in dynamic perspective, taking into consideration the experience of the last fifty years in respect of its intended and unintended consequences. The desirability or otherwise of descheduling individuals/communities who have registered an advance during this period should receive serious consideration.[24] However, quest for social justice with the help of constitutional and legal means has its limitations. Therefore, social intervention and action may also help us to achieve the goal of social justice in the true sense of the term.[25] Speaking at Antyaja Conference and Untouchability Conference what Mahatma Gandhi had said was worth considering even today. He said, "....But do not believe that all class distinctions can be obliterated. I believe in the doctrine of equality as taught by Lord Kirshna in the *Gita*. The *Gita* teaches us that members of all the four castes should be treated on an equal basis. It does not prescribe the same *dharma* for the Brahmin as for the Bhangi. But it insists that the latter shall be entitled to the same measure of consideration and esteem as the former with all his superior learning."[26]

REFERENCES

1. See Shashi, S.S. (Eds.), *Ambedkar and Social Justice*, Publications Division, Ministry of Information and Broadcasting, Govt. of India, New Delhi, 1992, p. 26.
2. *Ibid.*
3. *Ibid.*, p. 27.

4. Narayan J., "Caste Violence and Dalits of Bihar," *The Hindustan Times*, (Monday Extra), Patna, Dec. 23, 1996, p. 3.
5. Lokhande, G.S., Bhim Rao Ramji Ambedkar: *A Study in Social Democracy*, Intellectual Publishing House, New Delhi, 1977, p. 161.
6. Rao, J. Laxminarasima, "Reservation Policy and the Principle of Merit: A Study of Indian Bureaucracy," *The Indian Journal of Political Science*, Vol. LIII, No. 4, Political Science Association, Madras, Oct.-Dec. 1992, pp. 479-80.
7. Ambedkar, B.R., *What Congress and Gandhi have done to Untouchables*?, Thacker and Co. Ltd, Bombay, 1945, p. 194.
8. Bains, Ravinder Singh, *Reservation Policy and Anti-Reservationists*, B.R. Publishing Corporation, Delhi, 1994, p.10.
9. Kamble, J.R., *Rise and Awakening of Depressed Classes in India*, National Publishing House, 1979, p.15.
10. Bains, Ravinder Singh, *op. cit.*, p. 9.
11. Lokhande, G.S., *op. cit.*, p. 163.
12. *Ibid.*, p. 161.
13. India, *Constituent Assembly Debates*, Vol. XI, p. 979.
14. *Ibid.*
15. See Mazumdar, Devaprasad, Sen, "The Weak and the Strong" in Hasnain, N., *Weaker Sections: The Psycho-Social Perspective,* Gyan Publishing House, New Delhi, 1998, p. 37.
16. Narayan, J., "Caste Violence in Bihar", *Indian Journal of Politics,* Vol. XXIX, Nos. 1-2, Aligarh Muslim University, Aligarh, 1995, p. 68.
17. Sachchidananda, "Reservation", Seminar No. 250, New Delhi, June 1980, p. 28.
18. Blair, Harry W., *Voting, Caste, Community, Society,* Young Asia Publications, New Delhi, 1979, p. 12; also see *The Indian Express,* New Delhi, Jan. 25, 1987; also see Singh, Janak, "Bihar continues to reel under orgies of violence", *The Times of India,* New Delhi, Feb. 15, 1994, p. 4; also see Singh, Nand Kishore, "Bhathani Tola Jansanghar", *Deskal* (Hindi), Delhi, Aug., 96, pp. 32-34; also see *Hindustan* (Hindi Daily), Patna, Dec. 26, 1993, p. 1; also see *India Today,* New Delhi, Sept. 15, 1992, p. 54.
19. See Rath, Rajlaxmi, "Social Transformation among Scheduled Castes in Bihar due to Job Reservation—A Case Study of Three Generation in Bihar*.
20. See Lal, A.K., "*Protective Discrimination: Social Necessity or Political Compulsions*?"*
21. See Sachchidananda, "Rethinking Scheduled Caste Reservation".*
22. See Mazumdar, Deva Prasad, Sen, *op. cit.*, p. 46.
23. Randadive, B.T., "Place of Ideology in Marxist Theory of Social Change",

* Papers presented at the National Seminar on *Protective Discrimination: Ideology and Praxis*, G.B. Pant Social Science Institute, Allahabad, March 24-25, 1998.

In Social Change in India, Social Scientist Marx Centenary Volume I, Social Scientist Press, Trivandrum, p. 15.

24. See Sachchidananda, *op. cit.*
25. See Singh R.R., "Social Intervention for Social Justice", paper presented at *National Seminar on Protective Discrimination: Ideology and Praxis*, G.B. Pant Social Science Institute, Allahabad, March 24-25, 1998.
26. Gandhi, M.K., *Hindu Dharma*, Navjivan Trust, Ahmedabad, 1991, pp. 102-107.

INDEX